G.a. Sussex 1861

BEACHY HEAD. &c.

BEACHY HEAD:

Harriet WITH *McClelland*

OTHER POEMS,

BY

CHARLOTTE SMITH.

NOW FIRST PUBLISHED.

———

LONDON:

PRINTED FOR THE AUTHOR;

AND SOLD BY J. JOHNSON, ST. PAUL'S
CHURCH-YARD.

1807.

W. Pople, Printer,
22, Old Boswell Court, Strand.

ADVERTISEMENT.

AS the following Poems were delivered to the Publisher as early as the month of May last, it may not be thought improper to state the circumstances that have hitherto delayed their appearance.

The fulfilling this duty to the public has since devolved to other hands; for alas! the admired author is now unconscious of their praise or censure, having fallen a victim to a long and painful illness, on the 28th of October last.

The delay which since that period has taken place, has been occasioned partly by the hope of finding a preface to the present publication, which there was some reason to suppose herself had written, and partly from an intention of annexing a short account of her life; but it having been since decided to publish biographical memoirs, and a selection of her correspondence, on a more enlarged plan, and under the immediate authority of her own nearest relatives, it was thought unnecessary; and the motives for deferring the publication are altogether removed.

The public, who have received the several editions of Mrs. Smith's former Poems with unbounded approbation, will, without doubt, admit the claims of the present work to an equal share of their favour; and her friends and admirers cannot fail of being highly gratified in observing, that although most of the Poems included in this volume were composed during the few and short intervals of care which her infirmities permitted her to enjoy; yet they bear the most unquestionable evidence of the same undiminished genius, spirit, and imagination, which so imminently distinguished her former productions.

The Poem entitled BEACHY HEAD is not completed according to the original design. That the increasing debility of its author has been the cause of its being left in an imperfect state, will it is hoped be a sufficient apology.

There are two Poems in this collection, viz. FLORA, and STUDIES BY THE SEA, which have already been published in Mrs. Smith's

" Conversations for the Use of Children and Young Persons"; but as many of her friends considered them as misplaced in that work, and not likely to fall under the general observation of those who were qualified to appreciate their superior elegance and exquisite fancy, and had expressed a desire of seeing them transplanted into a more congenial soil, the Publisher, with his usual liberality, has permitted them to re-appear in the present volume.

January 31, 1807.

MISCELLANEOUS POEMS.

BEACHY HEAD.

On thy stupendous summit, rock sublime!
That o'er the channel rear'd, half way at sea
The mariner at early morning hails,
I would recline; while Fancy should go forth,
And represent the strange and awful hour
Of vast concussion; when the Omnipotent
Stretch'd forth his arm, and rent the solid hills,
Bidding the impetuous main flood rush between

B

The rifted shores, and from the continent
Eternally divided this green isle.
Imperial lord of the high southern coast!
From thy projecting head-land I would mark
Far in the east the shades of night disperse,
Melting and thinned, as from the dark blue wave
Emerging, brilliant rays of arrowy light
Dart from the horizon; when the glorious sun
Just lifts above it his resplendent orb.
Advances now, with feathery silver touched,
The rippling tide of flood; glisten the sands,
While, inmates of the chalky clefts that scar
Thy sides precipitous, with shrill harsh cry,
Their white wings glancing in the level beam,
The terns, and gulls, and tarrocks, seek their food,
And thy rough hollows echo to the voice

Of the gray choughs, and ever restless daws,
With clamour, not unlike the chiding hounds,
While the lone shepherd, and his baying dog,
Drive to thy turfy crest his bleating flock.

The high meridian of the day is past,
And Ocean now, reflecting the calm Heaven,
Is of cerulean hue; and murmurs low
The tide of ebb, upon the level sands.
The sloop, her angular canvas shifting still,
Catches the light and variable airs
That but a little crisp the summer sea,
Dimpling its tranquil surface.

Afar off,
And just emerging from the arch immense

Where seem to part the elements, a fleet
Of fishing vessels stretch their lesser sails;
While more remote, and like a dubious spot
Just hanging in the horizon, laden deep,
The ship of commerce richly freighted, makes
Her slower progress, on her distant voyage,
Bound to the orient climates, where the sun
Matures the spice within its odorous shell,
And, rivalling the gray worm's filmy toil,
Bursts from its pod the vegetable down;
Which in long turban'd wreaths, from torrid heat
Defends the brows of Asia's countless casts.
There the Earth hides within her glowing breast
The beamy adamant, and the round pearl
Enchased in rugged covering; which the slave,
With perilous and breathless toil, tears off

From the rough sea-rock, deep beneath the waves.
These are the toys of Nature; and her sport
Of little estimate in Reason's eye :
And they who reason, with abhorrence see
Man, for such gaudes and baubles, violate
The sacred freedom of his fellow man—
Erroneous estimate ! As Heaven's pure air,
Fresh as it blows on this aërial height,
Or sound of seas upon the stony strand,
Or inland, the gay harmony of birds,
And winds that wander in the leafy woods ;
Are to the unadulterate taste more worth
Than the elaborate harmony, brought out
From fretted stop, or modulated airs
Of vocal science.—So the brightest gems,
Glancing resplendent on the regal crown,

Or trembling in the high born beauty's ear,
Are poor and paltry, to the lovely light
Of the fair star, that as the day declines,
Attendant on her queen, the crescent moon,
Bathes her bright tresses in the eastern wave.
For now the sun is verging to the sea,
And as he westward sinks, the floating clouds
Suspended, move upon the evening gale,
And gathering round his orb, as if to shade
The insufferable brightness, they resign
Their gauzy whiteness ; and more warm'd, assume
All hues of purple.   There, transparent gold
Mingles with ruby tints, and sapphire gleams,
And colours, such as Nature through her works
Shews only in the ethereal canopy.
Thither aspiring Fancy fondly soars,

Wandering sublime thro' visionary vales,

Where bright pavilions rise, and trophies, fann'd

By airs celestial; and adorn'd with wreaths

Of flowers that bloom amid elysian bowers.

Now bright, and brighter still the colours glow,

Till half the lustrous orb within the flood

Seems to retire: the flood reflecting still

Its splendor, and in mimic glory drest;

Till the last ray shot upward, fires the clouds

With blazing crimson; then in paler light,

Long lines of tenderer radiance, lingering yield

To partial darkness; and on the opposing side

The early moon distinctly rising, throws

Her pearly brilliance on the trembling tide.

The fishermen, who at set seasons pass
Many a league off at sea their toiling night,
Now hail their comrades, from their daily task
Returning; and make ready for their own,
With the night tide commencing:—The night tide
Bears a dark vessel on, whose hull and sails
Mark her a coaster from the north. Her keel
Now ploughs the sand; and sidelong now she leans,
While with loud clamours her athletic crew
Unload her; and resounds the busy hum
Along the wave-worn rocks. Yet more remote,
Where the rough cliff hangs beetling o'er its base,
All breathes repose; the water's rippling sound
Scarce heard; but now and then the sea-snipe's cry
Just tells that something living is abroad;
And sometimes crossing on the moonbright line,

Glimmers the skiff, faintly discern'd awhile,

Then lost in shadow.

                    Contemplation here,

High on her throne of rock, aloof may sit,

And bid recording Memory unfold

Her scroll voluminous—bid her retrace

The period, when from Neustria's hostile shore

The Norman launch'd his galleys, and the bay

O'er which that mass of ruin frowns even now

In vain and sullen menace, then received

The new invaders; a proud martial race,

Of Scandinavia the undaunted sons,

Whom Dogon, Fier-a-bras, and Humfroi led

To conquest: while Trinacria to their power

Yielded her wheaten garland; and when thou,

Parthenope ! within thy fertile bay

Receiv'd the victors——

                In the mailed ranks

Of Normans landing on the British coast

Rode Taillefer ; and with astounding voice

Thunder'd the war song daring Roland sang

First in the fierce contention : vainly brave,

One not inglorious struggle England made——

But failing, saw the Saxon heptarchy

Finish for ever.——Then the holy pile,

Yet seen upon the field of conquest, rose,

Where to appease heaven's wrath for so much blood,

The conqueror bade unceasing prayers ascend,

And requiems for the slayers and the slain.

But let not modern Gallia form from hence

Presumptuous hopes, that ever thou again,

Queen of the isles! shalt crouch to foreign arms.

The enervate sons of Italy may yield;

And the Iberian, all his trophies torn

And wrapp'd in Superstition's monkish weed,

May shelter his abasement, and put on

Degrading fetters.   Never, never thou!

Imperial mistress of the obedient sea;

But thou, in thy integrity secure,

Shalt now undaunted meet a world in arms.

England! 'twas where this promontory rears

Its rugged brow above the channel wave,

Parting the hostile nations, that thy fame,

Thy naval fame was tarnish'd, at what time

Thou, leagued with the Batavian, gavest to France

One day of triumph—triumph the more loud,

Because even then so rare.   Oh! well redeem'd,

Since, by a series of illustrious men,

Such as no other country ever rear'd,

To vindicate her cause.   It is a list

Which, as Fame echoes it, blanches the cheek

Of bold Ambition ; while the despot feels

The extorted sceptre tremble in his grasp.

From even the proudest roll by glory fill'd,

How gladly the reflecting mind returns

To simple scenes of peace and industry,

Where, bosom'd in some valley of the hills

Stands the lone farm ; its gate with tawny ricks

Surrounded, and with granaries and sheds,

Roof'd with green mosses, and by elms and ash

Partially shaded; and not far remov'd

The hut of sea-flints built; the humble home

Of one, who sometimes watches on the heights,

When hid in the cold mist of passing clouds,

The flock, with dripping fleeces, are dispers'd

O'er the wide down; then from some ridged point

That overlooks the sea, his eager eye

Watches the bark that for his signal waits

To land its merchandize :—Quitting for this

Clandestine traffic his more honest toil,

The crook abandoning, he braves himself

The heaviest snow-storm of December's night,

When with conflicting winds the ocean raves,

And on the tossing boat, unfearing mounts

To meet the partners of the perilous trade,

And share their hazard.　Well it were for him,

If no such commerce of destruction known,

He were content with what the earth affords

To human labour; even where she seems

Reluctant most.   More happy is the hind,

Who, with his own hands rears on some black moor,

Or turbary, his independent hut

Cover'd with heather, whence the slow white smoke

Of smouldering peat arises————A few sheep,

His best possession, with his children share

The rugged shed when wintry tempests blow;

But, when with Spring's return the green blades rise

Amid the russet heath, the household live

Joint tenants of the waste throughout the day,

And often, from her nest, among the swamps,

Where the gemm'd sun-dew grows, or fring'd buck-bean,

They scare the plover, that with plaintive cries

Flutters, as sorely wounded, down the wind.

Rude, and but just remov'd from savage life

Is the rough dweller among scenes like these,

(Scenes all unlike the poet's fabling dreams

Describing Arcady)—But he is free;

The dread that follows on illegal acts

He never feels; and his industrious mate

Shares in his labour.   Where the brook is traced

By crouding osiers, and the black coot hides

Among the plashy reeds, her diving brood,

The matron wades; gathering the long green rush

That well prepar'd hereafter lends its light

To her poor cottage, dark and cheerless else

Thro' the drear hours of Winter.   Otherwhile

She leads her infant group where charlock grows

" Unprofitably gay,"   or to the fields,

Where congregate the linnet and the finch,
That on the thistles, so profusely spread,
Feast in the desert; the poor family
Early resort, extirpating with care
These, and the gaudier mischief of the ground;
Then flames the high rais'd heap; seen afar off
Like hostile war-fires flashing to the sky.
Another task is theirs: On fields that shew
As angry Heaven had rain'd sterility,
Stony and cold, and hostile to the plough,
Where clamouring loud, the evening curlew runs
And drops her spotted eggs among the flints;
The mother and the children pile the stones
In rugged pyramids;—and all this toil
They patiently encounter; well content
On their flock bed to slumber undisturb'd

Beneath the smoky roof they call their own.

Oh! little knows the sturdy hind, who stands

Gazing, with looks where envy and contempt

Are often strangely mingled, on the car

Where prosperous Fortune sits; what secret care

Or sick satiety is often hid,

Beneath the splendid outside: *He* knows not

How frequently the child of Luxury

Enjoying nothing, flies from place to place

In chase of pleasure that eludes his grasp;

And that content is e'en less found by him,

Than by the labourer, whose pick-axe smooths

The road before his chariot; and who doffs

What *was* an hat; and as the train pass on,

Thinks how one day's expenditure, like this,

c

Would cheer him for long months, when to his toil

The frozen earth closes her marble breast.

Ah! who *is* happy?   Happiness! a word

That like false fire, from marsh effluvia born,

Misleads the wanderer, destin'd to contend

In the world's wilderness, with want or woe

Yet *they* are happy, who have never ask'd

What good or evil means.   The boy

That on the river's margin gaily plays,

Has heard that Death is there—He knows not Death,

And therefore fears it not; and venturing in

He gains a bullrush, or a minnow—then,

At certain peril, for a worthless prize,

A crow's, or raven's nest, he climbs the boll

Of some tall pine; and of his prowess proud,

Is for a moment happy.   Are *your* cares,

Ye who despise him, never worse applied?

The village girl is happy, who sets forth

To distant fair, gay in her Sunday suit,

With cherry colour'd knots, and flourish'd shawl,

And bonnet newly purchas'd.   So is he

Her little brother, who his mimic drum

Beats, till he drowns her rural lovers' oaths

Of constant faith, and still increasing love;

Ah! yet a while, and half those oaths believ'd,

Her happiness is vanish'd; and the boy

While yet a stripling, finds the sound he lov'd

Has led him on, till he has given up

His freedom, and his happiness together.

_I_ once was happy, when while yet a child,

I learn'd to love these upland solitudes,

And, when elastic as the mountain air,

To my light spirit, care was yet unknown

And evil unforeseen:——Early it came,

And childhood scarcely passed, I was condemned,

A guiltless exile, silently to sigh,

While Memory, with faithful pencil, drew

The contrast; and regretting, I compar'd

With the polluted smoky atmosphere

And dark and stifling streets, the southern hills

That to the setting Sun, their graceful heads

Rearing, o'erlook the frith, where Vecta breaks

With her white rocks, the strong impetuous tide,

When western winds the vast Atlantic urge

To thunder on the coast——Haunts of my youth!

Scenes of fond day dreams, I behold ye yet!

Where 'twas so pleasant by thy northern slopes

To climb the winding sheep-path, aided oft

By scatter'd thorns: whose spiny branches bore

Small woolly tufts, spoils of the vagrant lamb

There seeking shelter from the noon-day sun ;

And pleasant, seated on the short soft turf,

To look beneath upon the hollow way

While heavily upward mov'd the labouring wain,

And stalking slowly by, the sturdy hind

To ease his panting team, stopp'd with a stone

The grating wheel.

           Advancing higher still

The prospect widens, and the village church

But little, o'er the lowly roofs around

Rears its gray belfry, and its simple vane;

Those lowly roofs of thatch are half conceal'd

By the rude arms of trees, lovely in spring,

When on each bough, the rosy-tinctur'd bloom

Sits thick, and promises autumnal plenty.

For even those orchards round the Norman farms,

Which, as their owners mark the promis'd fruit,

Console them for the vineyards of the south,

Surpass not these.

    Where woods of ash, and beech,

And partial copses, fringe the green hill foot,

The upland shepherd rears his modest home,.

There wanders by, a little nameless stream

That from the hill wells forth, bright now and clear,

Or after rain with chalky mixture gray,

But still refreshing in its shallow course,

The cottage garden; most for use design'd,

Yet not of beauty destitute.   The vine

Mantles the little casement; yet the briar

Drops fragrant dew among the July flowers;

And pansies rayed, and freak'd and mottled pinks

Grow among balm, and rosemary and rue:

There honeysuckles flaunt, and roses blow

Almost uncultured: Some with dark green leaves

Contrast their flowers of pure unsullied white;

Others, like velvet robes of regal state

Of richest crimson, while in thorny moss

Enshrined and cradled, the most lovely, wear

The hues of youthful beauty's glowing cheek.

With fond regret I recollect e'en now

In Spring and Summer, what delight I felt

Among these cottage gardens, and how much
Such artless nosegays, knotted with a rush
By village housewife or her ruddy maid,
Were welcome to me; soon and simply pleas'd.

An early worshipper at Nature's shrine,
I loved her rudest scenes—warrens, and heaths,
And yellow commons, and birch-shaded hollows,
And hedge rows, bordering unfrequented lanes
Bowered with wild roses, and the clasping woodbine
Where purple tassels of the tangling vetch
With bittersweet, and bryony inweave,
And the dew fills the silver bindweed's cups—
I loved to trace the brooks whose humid banks
Nourish the harebell, and the freckled pagil;
And stroll among o'ershadowing woods of beech,

Lending in Summer, from the heats of noon

A whispering shade ; while haply there reclines

Some pensive lover of uncultur'd flowers,

Who, from the tumps with bright green mosses clad,

Plucks the wood sorrel, with its light thin leaves,

Heart-shaped, and triply folded ; and its root

Creeping like beaded coral ; or who there

Gathers, the copse's pride, anémones,

With rays like golden studs on ivory laid

Most delicate : but touch'd with purple clouds,

Fit crown for April's fair but changeful brow.

Ah ! hills so early loved ! in fancy still

I breathe your pure keen air ; and still behold

Those widely spreading views, mocking alike

The Poet and the Painter's utmost art.

And still, observing objects more minute,
Wondering remark the strange and foreign forms
Of sea-shells ; with the pale calcareous soil
Mingled, and seeming of resembling substance.
Tho' surely the blue Ocean (from the heights
Where the downs westward trend, but dimly seen)
Here never roll'd its surge.   Does Nature then
Mimic, in wanton mood, fantastic shapes
Of bivalves, and inwreathed volutes, that cling
To the dark sea-rock of the wat'ry world ?
Or did this range of chalky mountains, once
Form a vast bason, where the Ocean waves
Swell'd fathomless? What time these fossil shells,
Buoy'd on their native-element, were thrown
Among the imbedding calx : when the huge hill
Its giant bulk heaved, and in strange ferment

Grew up a guardian barrier, 'twixt the sea
And the green level of the sylvan weald.

Ah! very vain is Science' proudest boast,
And but a little light its flame yet lends
To its most ardent votaries; since from whence
These fossil forms are seen, is but conjecture,
Food for vague theories, or vain dispute,
While to his daily task the peasant goes,
Unheeding such inquiry; with no care
But that the kindly change of sun and shower,
Fit for his toil the earth he cultivates.
As little recks the herdsman of the hill,
Who on some turfy knoll, idly reclined,
Watches his wether flock; that deep beneath
Rest the remains of men, of whom is left

No traces in the records of mankind,

Save what these half obliterated mounds

And half fill'd trenches doubtfully impart

To some lone antiquary; who on times remote,

Since which two thousand years have roll'd away,

Loves to contemplate. He perhaps may trace,

Or fancy he can trace, the oblong square

Where the mail'd legions, under Claudius, rear'd

The rampire, or excavated fossé delved ;

What time the huge unwieldy Elephant

Auxiliary reluctant, hither led,

From Afric's forest glooms and tawny sands,

First felt the Northern blast, and his vast frame

Sunk useless ; whence in after ages found,

The wondering hinds, on those enormous bones

Gaz'd; and in giants dwelling on the hills

Believed and marvell'd—

Hither, Ambition, come!

Come and behold the nothingness of all

For which you carry thro' the oppressed Earth,

War, and its train of horrors—see where tread

The innumerous hoofs of flocks above the works

By which the warrior sought to register

His glory, and immortalize his name—

The pirate Dane, who from his circular camp

Bore in destructive robbery, fire and sword

Down thro' the vale, sleeps unremember'd here;

And here, beneath the green sward, rests alike

The savage native, who his acorn meal

Shar'd with the herds, that ranged the pathless woods;

And the centurion, who on these wide hills

Encamping, planted the Imperial Eagle.

All, with the lapse of Time, have passed away,

Even as the clouds, with dark and dragon shapes,
Or like vast promontories crown'd with towers,
Cast their broad shadows on the downs : then sail
Far to the northward, and their transient gloom
Is soon forgotten.

              But from thoughts like these,
By human crimes suggested, let us turn
To where a more attractive study courts
The wanderer of the hills ; while shepherd girls
Will from among the fescue bring him flowers,
Of wonderous mockery ; some resembling bees
In velvet vest, intent on their sweet toil,
While others mimic flies, that lightly sport
In the green shade, or float along the pool,
But here seem perch'd upon the slender stalk,

And gathering honey dew.   While in the breeze
That wafts the thistle's plumed seed along,
Blue bells wave tremulous.   The mountain thyme
Purples the hassock of the heaving mole,
And the short turf is gay with tormentil,
And bird's foot trefoil, and the lesser tribes
Of hawkweed; spangling it with fringed stars.—
Near where a richer tract of cultur'd land
Slopes to the south; and burnished by the sun,
Bend in the gale of August, floods of corn;
The guardian of the flock, with watchful care,
Repels by voice and dog the encroaching sheep—
While his boy visits every wired trap
That scars the turf; and from the pit-falls takes
The timid migrants, who from distant wilds,
Warrens, and stone quarries, are destined thus

To lose their short existence.   But unsought

By Luxury yet, the Shepherd still protects

The social bird, who from his native haunts

Of willowy current, or the rushy pool,

Follows the fleecy croud, and flirts and skims,

In fellowship among them.

                      Where the knoll

More elevated takes the changeful winds,

The windmill rears its vanes ; and thitherward

With his white load, the master travelling,

Scares the rooks rising slow on whispering wings,

While o'er his head, before the summer sun

Lights up the blue expanse, heard more than seen,

The lark sings matins ; and above the clouds

Floating, embathes his spotted breast in dew.

Beneath the shadow of a gnarled thorn,

Bent by the sea blast, from a seat of turf

With fairy nosegays strewn, how wide the view !

Till in the distant north it melts away,

And mingles indiscriminate with clouds :

But if the eye could reach so far, the mart

Of England's capital, its domes and spires

Might be perceived—Yet hence the distant range

Of Kentish hills, appear in purple haze ;

And nearer, undulate the wooded heights,

And airy summits, that above the mole

Rise in green beauty ; and the beacon'd ridge

Of Black-down shagg'd with heath, and swelling rude

Like a dark island from the vale ; its brow

Catching the last rays of the evening sun

That gleam between the nearer park's old oaks,

D

Then lighten up the river, and make prominent
The portal, and the ruin'd battlements
Of that dismantled fortress ; rais'd what time
 The Conqueror's successors fiercely fought,
Tearing with civil feuds the desolate land.
But now a tiller of the soil dwells there,
And of the turret's loop'd and rafter'd halls
Has made an humbler homestead——Where he sees,
Instead of armed foemen, herds that graze
Along his yellow meadows ; or his flocks
At evening from the upland driv'n to fold——

In such a castellated mansion once
A stranger chose his home ; and where hard by
In rude disorder fallen, and hid with brushwood
Lay fragments gray of towers and buttresses,

Among the ruins, often he would muse—

His rustic meal soon ended, he was wont

To wander forth, listening the evening sounds

Of rushing milldam, or the distant team,

Or night-jar, chasing fern-flies : the tir'd hind

Pass'd him at nightfall, wondering he should sit

On the hill top so late : they from the coast

Who sought bye paths with their clandestine load,

Saw with suspicious doubt, the lonely man

Cross on their way : but village maidens thought

His senses injur'd ; and with pity say

That he, poor youth ! must have been cross'd in love—

For often, stretch'd upon the mountain turf

With folded arms, and eyes intently fix'd

Where ancient elms and firs obscured a grange,

Some little space within the vale below,

D 2

They heard him, as complaining of his fate,
And to the murmuring wind, of cold neglect
And baffled hope he told.——The peasant girls
These plaintive sounds remember, and even now
Among them may be heard the stranger's songs.

———

Were I a Shepherd on the hill
    And ever as the mists withdrew
Could see the willows of the rill
Shading the footway to the mill
    Where once I walk'd with you——

And as away Night's shadows sail,
   And sounds of birds and brooks arise,
Believe, that from the woody vale
I hear your voice upon the gale
   In soothing melodies ;

And viewing from the Alpine height,
   The prospect dress'd in hues of air,
Could say, while transient colours bright
Touch'd the fair scene with dewy light,
   'Tis, that *her* eyes are there!

I think, I could endure my lot
   And linger on a few short years,
And then, by all but you forgot,
Sleep, where the turf that clothes the spot
   May claim some pitying tears.

For 'tis not easy to forget
    One, who thro' life has lov'd you still,
And you, however late, might yet
With sighs to Memory giv'n, regret
    The Shepherd of the Hill.

Yet otherwhile it seem'd as if young Hope
Her flattering pencil gave to Fancy's hand,
And in his wanderings, rear'd to sooth his soul
Ideal bowers of pleasure——Then, of Solitude
And of his hermit life, still more enamour'd,
His home was in the forest; and wild fruits

And bread sustain'd him.   There in early spring
The Barkmen found him, e'er the sun arose ;
There at their daily toil, the Wedgecutters
Beheld him thro' the distant thicket move.
The shaggy dog following the truffle hunter,
Bark'd at the loiterer ; and perchance at night
Belated villagers from fair or wake,
While the fresh night-wind let the moonbeams in
Between the swaying boughs, just saw him pass,
And then in silence, gliding like a ghost
He vanish'd ! Lost among the deepening gloom.—
But near one ancient tree, whose wreathed roots
Form'd a rude couch, love-songs and scatter'd rhymes,
Unfinish'd sentences, or half erased,
And rhapsodies like this, were sometimes found—

Let us to woodland wilds repair
   While yet the glittering night-dews seem
To wait the freshly-breathing air,
   Precursive of the morning beam,
That rising with advancing day,
Scatters the silver drops away.

An elm, uprooted by the storm,
   The trunk with mosses gray and green,
Shall make for us a rustic form,
   Where lighter grows the forest scene ;
And far among the bowery shades,
Are ferny lawns and grassy glades.

Retiring May to lovely June
   Her latest garland now resigns ;
The banks with cuckoo-flowers are strewn,
   The woodwalks blue with columbines,
And with its reeds, the wandering stream
Reflects the flag-flower's golden gleam.

There, feathering down the turf to meet,
   Their shadowy arms the beeches spread,
While high above our sylvan seat,
   Lifts the light ash its airy head ;
And later leaved, the oaks between
Extend their bows of vernal green.

The slender birch its paper rind
    Seems offering to divided love,
And shuddering even without a wind
    Aspins, their paler foliage move,
As if some spirit of the air
Breath'd a low sigh in passing there.

The Squirrel in his frolic mood,
    Will fearless bound among the boughs;
Yaffils laugh loudly thro' the wood,
    And murmuring ring-doves tell their vows;
While we, as sweetest woodscents rise,
Listen to woodland melodies.

And I'll contrive a sylvan room
  Against the time of summer heat,
Where leaves, inwoven in Nature's loom,
  Shall canopy our green retreat ;
And gales that " close the eye of day"
Shall linger, e'er they die away.

And when a sear and sallow hue
  From early frost the bower receives,
I'll dress the sand rock cave for you,
  And strew the floor with heath and leaves,
That you, against the autumnal air
May find securer shelter there.

The Nightingale will then have ceas'd
   To sing her moonlight serenade ;
But the gay bird with blushing breast,
   And Woodlarks still will haunt the shade,
And by the borders of the spring
Reed-wrens will yet be carolling.

The forest hermit's lonely cave
   None but such soothing sounds shall reach,
Or hardly heard, the distant wave
   Slow breaking on the stony beach ;
Or winds, that now sigh soft and low,
Now make wild music as they blow.

And then, before the chilling North
   The tawny foliage falling light,
Seems, as it flits along the earth,
   The footfall of the busy Sprite,
Who wrapt in pale autumnal gloom,
Calls up the mist-born Mushroom.

Oh ! could I hear your soft voice there,
   And see you in the forest green
All beauteous as you are, more fair
   You 'ld look, amid the sylvan scene,
And in a wood-girl's simple guise,
Be still more lovely in mine eyes.

Ye phantoms of unreal delight,
      Visions of fond delirium born!
Rise not on my deluded sight,
      Then leave me drooping and forlorn
To know, such bliss can never be,
Unless   loved like me.

The visionary, nursing dreams like these,
Is not indeed unhappy.   Summer woods
Wave over him, and whisper as they wave,
Some future blessings he may yet enjoy.
And as above him sail the silver clouds,
He follows them in thought to distant climes,
Where, far from the cold policy of this,

Dividing him from her he fondly loves,

He, in some island of the southern sea,

May haply build his cane-constructed bower

Beneath the bread-fruit, or aspiring palm,

With long green foliage rippling in the gale.

Oh! let him cherish his ideal bliss——

For what is life, when Hope has ceas'd to strew

Her fragile flowers along its thorny way?

And sad and gloomy are his days, who lives

Of Hope abandon'd!

     Just beneath the rock

Where Beachy overpeers the channel wave,

Within a cavern mined by wintry tides

Dwelt one, who long disgusted with the world

And all its ways, appear'd to suffer life

Rather than live ; the soul-reviving gale,

Fanning the bean-field, or the thymy heath,

Had not for many summers breathed on him ;

And nothing mark'd to him the season's change,

Save that more gently rose the placid sea,

And that the birds which winter on the coast

Gave place to other migrants; save that the fog,

Hovering no more above the beetling cliffs

Betray'd not then the little careless sheep

On the brink grazing, while their headlong fall

Near the lone Hermit's flint-surrounded home,

Claim'd unavailing pity ; for his heart

Was feelingly alive to all that breath'd ;

And outraged as he was, in sanguine youth,

By human crimes, he still acutely felt

For human misery.

Wandering on the beach,
He learn'd to augur from the clouds of heaven,
And from the changing colours of the sea,
And sullen murmurs of the hollow cliffs,
Or the dark porpoises, that near the shore
Gambol'd and sported on the level brine
When tempests were approaching : then at night
He listen'd to the wind; and as it drove
The billows with o'erwhelming vehemence
He, starting from his rugged couch, went forth
And hazarding a life, too valueless,
He waded thro' the waves, with plank or pole.
Towards where the mariner in conflict dread
Was buffeting for life the roaring surge ;
And now just seen, now lost in foaming gulphs,
The dismal gleaming of the clouded moon

E

Shew'd the dire peril.   Often he had snatch'd
From the wild billows, some unhappy man
Who liv'd to bless the hermit of the rocks.
But if his generous cares were all in vain,
And with slow swell the tide of morning bore
Some blue swol'n cor'se to land; the pale recluse
Dug in the chalk a sepulchre—above
Where the dank sea-wrack mark'd the utmost tide,
And with his prayers perform'd the obsequies
For the poor helpless stranger.

                        One dark night
The equinoctial wind blew south by west,
Fierce on the shore;—the bellowing cliffs were shook
Even to their stony base, and fragments fell
Flashing and thundering on the angry flood.

At day-break, anxious for the lonely man,

His cave the mountain shepherds visited,

Tho' sand and banks of weeds had choak'd their way—

He was not in it; but his drowned cor'se

By the waves wafted, near his former home

Receiv'd the rites of burial.   Those who read

Chisel'd within the rock, these mournful lines,

Memorials of his sufferings, did not grieve,

That dying in the cause of charity

His spirit, from its earthly bondage freed,

Had to some better region fled for ever.

THE TRUANT DOVE,

FROM PILPAY.

A FABLE.

A MOUNTAIN stream, its channel deep
Beneath a rock's rough base had torn;
The cliff, like a vast castle wall, was steep
By fretting rains in many a crevice worn;
But the fern wav'd there, and the mosses crept,
And o'er the summit, where the wind
Peel'd from their stems the silver rind,
Depending birches wept——
There, tufts of broom a footing used to find,

And heath and straggling grass to grow,

And half-way down from roots enwreathing, broke

The branches of a scathed oak,

And seem'd to guard the cave below,

Where each revolving year,

Their twins, two faithful doves were wont to rear;

Choice never join'd a fonder pair;

To each their simple home was dear,

No discord ever enter'd there;

But there the soft affections dwell'd,

And three returning springs beheld

Secure within their fortress high

The little happy family.

" Toujours perdrix, messieurs, ne valent rien"—

So did a Gallic monarch once harangue,

And evil was the day whereon our bird

This saying heard,

From certain new acquaintance he had found,

Who at their perfect ease,

Amid a field of peas

Boasted to him, that all the country round,

The wheat, and oats, and barley, rye and tares,

Quite to the neighbouring sea, were theirs;

And theirs the oak, and beech-woods, far and near,

For their right noble owner was a peer,

And they themselves, luxuriantly were stored

In a great dove-cote—to amuse my lord!

" Toujours perdrix ne valent rien." 'That's strange

When people once are happy, wherefore change?

So thought our stock-dove, but communication,

With birds in his new friend's exalted station,

Whose means of information,

And knowledge of all sorts, must be so ample ;
Who saw great folks, and follow'd their example,
Made on the dweller of the cave, impression;
And soon, whatever was his best possession,
His sanctuary within the rock's deep breast,
His soft-eyed partner, and her nest,
He thought of with indifference, then with loathing ;
So much insipid love was good for nothing.—
But sometimes tenderness return'd; his dame
So long belov'd, so mild, so free from blame,
How should he tell her, he had learn'd to cavil
At happiness itself, and longed to travel ?
His heart still smote him, so much wrong to do her,
He knew not how to break the matter to her.
But love, tho' blind himself, makes some discerning ;
His frequent absence, and his late returning,

With ruffled plumage, and with alter'd eyes,

His careless short replies,

And to their couplets, coldness or neglect

Had made his gentle wife suspect,

All was not right; but she forbore to teaze him,

Which would but give him an excuse to rove:

She therefore tried by every art to please him,

Endur'd his peevish starts with patient love,

And when (like other husbands from a tavern)

Of his new notions full, he sought his cavern

She with dissembled cheerfulness, "beguiled

" The thing she was," and gaily coo-ed and smiled.

'Tis not in this most motley sphere uncommon,

For man, (and so of course more feeble woman)

Most strongly to suspect, what they're pursuing

Will lead them to inevitable ruin,

Yet rush with open eyes to their undoing;

Thus felt the dove; but in the cant of fashion

He talk'd of fate, and of predestination,

And in a grave oration,

He to his much affrighted mate related,

How he, yet slumbering in the egg, was fated,

To gather knowledge, to instruct his kind,

By observation elevate his mind,

And give new impulse to Columbian life;

" If it be so," exclaim'd his hapless wife,

" It is *my* fate, to pass my days in pain,

" To mourn your love estrang'd, and mourn in vain;

" Here in our once dear hut, to wake and weep,

" When thy unkindness shall have 'murder'd sleep;'

" And never that dear hut shall I prepare,

" And wait with fondness your arrival there,

" While me, and mine forgetting, you will go

" To some new love."   " Why, *no*, I tell you *no*,—

" What shall I say such foolish fears to cure?

" I only mean to make a little tour,

" Just—just to see the world around me ; then

" With new delight, I shall come home again ;

" Such tours are quite the rage—at my return

" I shall have much to tell, and you to learn ;

" Of fashions—some becoming, some grotesque

" Of change of empires, and ideas novel ;

" Of buildings, Grecian, Gothic, Arabesque,

" And scenery sublime and picturesque ;

" And all these things with pleasure we'll discuss—"

" Ah, me ! and what are all these things to us ?"

" So then, you'd have a bird of genius grovel,

" And never see beyond a farmer's hovel ?

" Even the sand-martin, that inferior creature,

" Goes once a year abroad."   " It is *his* nature,

" But yours how different once !" and then she sigh'd,

" There *was* a time, Ah! would that I had died,

" E'er you so chang'd! when you'd have perish'd rather

" Than this poor breast should heave a single feather

" With grief and care.   And all this cant of fashion

" Would but have rais'd your anger, or compassion,—

" O my dear love! You sought not then to range,

" But on my changeful neck as fell the light,

" You sweetly said, you wish'd no other change

" Than that soft neck could shew ; to berries bright

" Of mountain ash, you fondly could compare

" My scarlet feet and bill ; my shape and air,

" Ah! faithless flatterer, did you not declare

" The soul of grace and beauty center'd there !

" My eyes you said, were opals, brightly pink,

" Enchas'd in onyx ; and you seem'd to think,

" Each charm might then the coldest heart enthrall :

" Those charms were mine. Alas ! I gave you all—

" Your farthest wanderings then were but to fetch

" The pea, the tare, the beechmast, and the vetch,

" For my repast ; within my rocky bower,

" With spleenwort shaded, and the blue-bell's flower,

" For prospects then you never wish'd to roam,

" But the best scenery was our happy home ;

" And when, beneath my breast, then fair and young,

" Our first dear pair, our earliest nestlings sprung,

" And weakly, indistinctly, tried to coo—

" Were not those moments picturesque to you ?"

" Yes, faith, my dear ; and all you say is true."

" Oh ! hear me then ; if thus we have been blest,

" If on these wings it was your joy to rest,

" Love must from habit still new strength be gaining—"

" From habit? 'tis of that, child, I'm complaining :

" This everlasting fondness will not be

" For birds of flesh and blood.   We sha'nt agree,

" So why dispute ? now prithee don't torment me ;

" I shall not long be gone ; let that content ye :

" Pshaw! what a fuss! Come, no more sighs and groans,

" Keep up your spirits ; mind your little ones ;

" My journey won't be far—my honour's pledged—

" I shall be back again before they're fledged ;

" Give me a kiss ; and now my dear, adieu !"

So light of heart and plumes, away he flew ;

And, as above the sheltering rock he springs,

She listen'd to the echo of his wings ;

Those well-known sounds, so soothing heretofore,

Which her heart whisper'd she should hear no more.

Then to her cold and widow'd bed she crept,

Clasp'd her half-orphan'd young, and wept!

Her recreant mate, by other views attracted,

A very different part enacted ;

He sought the dove-cote, and was greeted there

With all that's tonish, elegant, and rare,

Among the pigeon tribes ; and there the rover

Lived quite in clover !

His jolly comrades now, were blades of spirit ;

Their nymphs possess'd most *fascinating* merit ;

Nor fail'd our hero of the rock to prove,

He thought not of inviolable love

To his poor spouse at home.   He bow'd and sigh'd,

Now to a fantail's, now a cropper's bride ;

Then cow'ring low to a majestic powter,
Declared he should not suffer life without her;
And then with upturn'd eyes, in phrase still humbler,
Implor'd the pity of an almond tumbler;
Next, to a beauteous carrier's feet he'd run,
And lived a week, the captive of a nun:
Thus far in measureless content he revels,
And blest the hour when he began his travels.
Yet some things soon occurr'd not quite so pleasant;
He had observ'd that an unfeeling peasant,
It silence mounting on a ladder high,
Seiz'd certain pigeons just as they could fly,
Who never figur'd more, but in a pie;
That was but aukward; then, his lordship's son
Heard from the groom, that 'twould be famous fun
To try on others his unpractis'd gun;

Their fall, the rattling shot, his nerves perplex'd ;

He thought perhaps it might be his turn next.

It has been seen ere now, that, much elated,

To be by some great man caress'd and fêted,

A youth of humble birth, and mind industrious,

Foregoes in evil hour his independance ;

And, charm'd to wait upon his friend illustrious,

Gives up his time to flattery and attendance.

His patron, smiling at his folly, lets him—

Some newer whim succeeds, and he forgets him.

So fared our bird ; his new friend's vacant stare,

Told him he scarce remember'd he was there ;

And, when he talk'd of living more securely,

This very dear friend, yawning, answered, " Surely !

" You are quite right to do what's most expedient,

" So, au revoir !—Good bye! Your most obedient."

Allies in prosperous fortune thus he prov'd,

And left them, unregretting, unbelov'd;

Yet much his self-love suffer'd by the shock,

And now, his quiet cabin in the rock,

The faithful partner of his every care,

And all the blessings he abandon'd there,

Rush'd on his sickening heart; he felt it yearn,

But pride and shame prevented his return;

So wandering farther—at the close of day

To the high woods he pensive wing'd his way;

But new distress at every turn he found—

Struck by an hawk, and stunn'd upon the ground,

He once by miracle escaped; then fled

From a wild cat, and hid his trembling head

Beneath a dock; recovering, on the wind

He rose once more, and left his fears behind;

And, as above the clouds he soar'd, the light
Fell on an inland rock ; the radiance bright
Shew'd him his long deserted place of rest,
And thitherward he flew ; his throbbing breast
Dwelt on his mate, so gentle, and so wrong'd,
And on his memory throng'd
The happiness he once at home had known ;
Then to forgive him earnest to engage her,
And for his errors eager to atone,
Onward he went ; but ah ! not yet had flown
Fate's sharpest arrow : to decide a wager,
Two sportsmen shot at our deserter ; down
The wind swift wheeling, struggling, still he fell,
Close to the margin of the stream that flow'd
Beneath the foot of his regretted cell,
And the fresh grass was spotted with his blood ;

To his dear home he turn'd his languid view,

Deplor'd his folly, while he look'd his last,

And sigh'd a long adieu !

Thither to sip the brook, his nestlings, led

By their still pensive mother, came ;

He saw ; and murmuring forth her dear lov'd name,

Implor'd her pity, and with shortening breath,

Besought her to forgive him ere his death.—

And now, how hard in metre to relate

The tears and tender pity of his mate !

Or with what generous zeal, his faithful moitie

Taught her now feather'd young, with duteous piety,

To aid her, on their mutual wings to bear,

With stork-like care,

Their suffering parent to the rock above ;

There, by the best physician, Love,

His wounds were heal'd.—His wanderings at an end,

And sober'd quite, the husband, and the friend,

In proof of reformation and contrition,

Gave to his race this prudent admonition ;

Advice, which this, our fabling muse, presumes

May benefit the *biped without plumes* :

" If of domestic peace you are possess'd,

" Learn to believe yourself supremely bless'd ;

" And gratefully enjoying your condition,

" Frisk not about, on whims and fancies strange,

" For ten to one, you for the worse will change ;

" And 'tis most wise, to check all vain ambition——

" By such aspiring pride the angels fell ;

" So love your wife, and know when you are well."

THE LARK's NEST.

A FABLE FROM ESOP.

" Trust only to thyself;" the maxim's sound

For, tho' life's choicest blessing be a friend,

Friends do not very much abound ;

Or, where they happen to be found,

And greatly thou on *friendship* shouldst depend,

Thou'lt find it will not bear

Much wear and tear ;

Nay ! that even kindred, cousin, uncle, brother,

Has each perhaps to mind his own affair ;

Attend to thine then ; lean not on another.

Esop assures us that the maxim's wise;

And by a tale illustrates his advice :

When April's bright and fickle beams

Saw every feather'd pair

In the green woodlands, or by willowy streams,

Busied in matrimonial schemes;

A Lark, amid the dewy air,

Woo'd, and soon won a favourite fair ;

And, in a spot by springing rye protected,

Her labour sometimes shared ;

While she, with bents, and wither'd grass collected,

Their humble domicile prepared ;

Then, by her duty fix'd, the tender mate

Unwearied prest

Their future progeny beneath her breast ;

And little slept, and little ate,

While her gay lover, with a careless heart,

As is the custom of his sex,

Full little recks

The coming family ; but like a dart,

From his low homested, with the morning springs ;

And far above the floating vapour, sings

At such an height,

That even the shepherd-lad upon the hill,

Hearing his matin note so shrill,

With shaded eyes against the lustre bright,

Scarce sees him twinkling in a flood of light.

But hunger, spite of all her perseverance,

Was one day urgent on his patient bride ;

The truant made not his appearance,

That her fond care might be a while supplied,—

So, because hunger will not be denied,

She leaves her nest reluctant ; and in haste

But just allows herself to taste,

A dew drop, and a few small seeds—

Ah ! how her fluttering bosom bleeds,

When the dear cradle she had fondly rear'd

All desolate appear'd !

And ranging wide about the field she saw

A setter huge, whose unrelenting jaw

Had crush'd her half-existing young ;

Long o'er her ruin'd hopes the mother hung,

And vainly mourn'd,

Ere from the clouds her wanderer return'd :—

Tears justly shed by beauty, who can stand them ?

He heard her plaintive tale with unfeign'd sorrow,

But, as his motto was, " Nil desperandum,"

Bade her hope better fortune for to-morrow ;

Then from the fatal spot afar, they sought

A safer shelter, having bought

Experience, which is always rather dear ;

And very near

A grassy headland, in a field of wheat,

They fix'd, with cautious care, their second seat—

But this took time ; May was already past,

The white thorn had her silver blossoms cast,

And there the Nightingale, to lovely June,

Her last farewell had sung ;

No longer reign'd July's intemperate noon,

And high in heaven the reaper's moon,

A little crescent hung,

Ere from their shells appear'd the plumeless young.

Oh! then with how much tender care,

The busy pair,

Watch'd and provided for the panting brood!

For then, the vagrant of the air,

Soar'd not to meet the morning star,

But, never from the nestlings far,

Explor'd each furrow, every sod for food;

While his more anxious partner tried

From hostile eyes, the helpless group to hide;

Attempting now, with labouring bill, to guide

The enwreathing bindweed round the nest;

Now joy'd to see the cornflower's azure crest

Above it waving, and the cockle grow,

Or poppies throw

Their scarlet curtains round;

While the more humble children of the ground,

Freak'd pansies, fumitory, pimpernel,

Circled with arras light, the secret cell :—

But who against all evils can provide?

Hid, and overshadow'd thus, and fortified,

By teasel, and the scabious' thready disk,

Corn-marygold. and thistles ; too much risk

The little household still were doom'd to run,

For the same ardent sun,

Whose beams had drawn up many an idle flower,

To fence the lonely bower,

Had by his powerful heat,

Matured the wheat ;

And chang'd of hue, it hung its heavy head,

While every rustling gale that blew along

From neighbouring uplands, brought the rustic song

Of harvest merriment : then full of dread,

Lest, not yet fully fledg'd, her race

The reaper's foot might crush, or reaper's dog might trace,

Or village child, too young to reap or bind,

Loitering around, her hidden treasure find ;

The mother bird was bent

To move them, e'er the sickle came more near ;

And therefore, when for food abroad she went,

(For now her mate again was on the ramble)

She bade her young report what they should hear :

So the next hour they cried, " They'll all assemble,

" The farmer's neighbours, with the dawn of light,

" Therefore, dear mother, let us move to night."

" Fear not, my loves," said she, " you need not tremble;

" Trust me, if only neighbours are in question,

" Eat what I bring, and spoil not your digestion

" Or sleep, for this."   Next day away she flew,

And that no neighbour came was very true;
But her returning wings the Larklings knew,
And quivering round her, told, their landlord said,
" Why, John ! the reaping must not be delay'd,
" By peep of day to-morrow we'll begin,
" Since now so many of our kin
" Have promis'd us their help to set about it."
" Still," quoth the bird, " I doubt it ;
" The corn will stand to-morrow."   So it prov'd ;
The morning's dawn arriv'd—but never saw
Or uncle, cousin, brother, or brother-in-law;
And not a reap-hook mov'd !
Then to his son the angry farmer cried,
" Some folks are little known 'till they are tried ;
" Who would have thought we had so few well-wishers!
" What ! neither neighbour Dawes, nor cousin Fishers,

" Nor uncle Betts, nor even my brother Delves,

" Will lend an hand, to help us get the corn in ?

" Well then, let you and me, to-morrow morning,

" E'en try what we can do with it ourselves."

" Nay," quoth the Lark, " 'tis time then to be gone :

" What a man undertakes himself is done."

Certes, she was a bird of observation ;

For very true it is, that none,

Whatever be his station,

Lord of a province, tenant of a mead,

Whether he fill a cottage, or a throne,

Or guard a flock, or guide a nation,

Is very likely to succeed,

Who manages affairs by deputation.

THE SWALLOW.

THE gorse is yellow on the heath,
   The banks with speedwell flowers are gay,
The oaks are budding ; and beneath,
The hawthorn soon will bear the wreath,
   The silver wreath of May.

The welcome guest of settled Spring,
   The Swallow too is come at last ;
Just at sun-set, when thrushes sing,
I saw her dash with rapid wing,
   And hail'd her as she pass'd.

THE SWALLOW.

Come, summer visitant, attach
  To my reed roof your nest of clay,
And let my ear your music catch
Low twittering underneath the thatch
  At the gray dawn of day.

As fables tell, an Indian Sage,
  The Hindostani woods among,
Could in his desert hermitage,
As if 'twere mark'd in written page,
  Translate the wild bird's song.

I wish I did his power possess,
  That I might learn, fleet bird, from thee,
What our vain systems only guess,
And know from what wide wilderness
  You came across the sea.

I would a little while restrain
   Your rapid wing, that I might hear
Whether on clouds that bring the rain,
You sail'd above the western main,
   The wind your charioteer.

In Afric, does the sultry gale
   Thro' spicy bower, and palmy grove,
Bear the repeated Cuckoo's tale?
Dwells *there* a time, the wandering Rail
   Or the itinerant Dove?

Were you in Asia? O relate,
   If there your fabled sister's woes
She seem'd in sorrow to narrate;
Or sings she but to celebrate
   Her nuptials with the rose?

G

I would enquire how journeying long,
    The vast and pathless ocean o'er,
You ply again those pinions strong,
And come to build anew among
    The scenes you left before ;

But if, as colder breezes blow,
    Prophetic of the waning year,
You hide, tho' none know when or how,
In the cliff's excavated brow,
    And linger torpid here ;

Thus lost to life, what favouring dream
    Bids you to happier hours awake;
And tells, that dancing in the beam,
The light gnat hovers o'er the stream,
    The May-fly on the lake ?

Or if, by instinct taught to know
　　Approaching dearth of insect food ;
To isles and willowy aits you go,
And crouding on the pliant bough,
　　Sink in the dimpling flood :

How learn ye, while the cold waves boom
　　Your deep and ouzy couch above,
The time when flowers of promise bloom,
And call you from your transient tomb,
　　To light, and life, and love ?

Alas ! how little can be known,
　　Her sacred veil where Nature draws ;
Let baffled Science humbly own,
Her mysteries understood alone,
　　By *Him* who gives her laws.

G 2

FLORA.

Remote from scenes, where the o'erwearied mind
Shrinks from the crimes and follies of mankind,
From hostile menace, and offensive boast,
Peace, and her train of home-born pleasures lost;
To fancy's reign, who would not gladly turn,
And lose awhile, the miseries they mourn
In sweet oblivion? Come then, Fancy! deign,
Queen of ideal pleasure, once again,
To lend thy magic pencil, and to bring
Such lovely forms, as in life's happier spring,

On the green margin of my native Wey,
Before mine infant eyes were wont to play,
And with that pencil, teach me to describe
The enchanting goddess of the flowery tribe,
Whose first prerogative it is to chase
The clouds that hang on languid beauty's face ;
And, while advancing suns and tepid showers,
Lead on the laughing Spring's delicious hours,
Bid the wan maid the hues of health assume,
Charm with new grace, and blush with fresher bloom.

The vision comes !—While slowly melt away,
Night's hovering shades before the eastern ray,
Ere yet declines the morning's humid star,
Fair Fancy brings her ; in her leafy car

Flora descends, to dress the expecting earth,
Awake the germs, and call the buds to birth ;
Bid each hybernacle its cell unfold,
And open silken leaves, and eyes of gold !

Of forest foliage of the firmest shade
Enwove by magic hands, the car was made ;
Oak, and the ample Plane, without entwined,
And Beech and Ash the verdant concave lin'd ;
The Saxifrage, that snowy flowers emboss,
Supplied the seat ; and of the mural moss
The velvet footstool rose, where lightly rest,
Her slender feet in Cypripedium drest.
The tufted rush, that bears a silken crown,
The floating feathers of the thistle's down,

In tender hues of rainbow lustre dyed,

The airy texture of her robe supplied,

And wild convolvuli, yet half unblown,

Form'd, with their wreathing buds, her simple zone ;

Some wandering tresses of her radiant hair,

Luxuriant floated on the enamour'd air ;

The rest were by the Scandix' points confin'd

And graced a shining knot, her head behind—

While, as a sceptre of supreme command,

She waved the Anthoxanthum in her hand.

Around the goddess, as the flies that play,

In countless myriads in the western ray,

The sylphs innumerous throng ; whose magic powers

Guard the soft buds, and nurse the infant flowers ;

Round the sustaining stems weak tendrils bind,

And save the pollen from dispersing wind ;

From suns too ardent, shade their transient hues,

And catch in odorous cups translucent dews.

The ruder tasks of others are, to chase

From vegetable life the insect race,

Break the polluting thread the spider weaves,

And brush the aphis from th' unfolding leaves.

For conquest arm'd these pigmy warriors wield

The thorny lance, and spread the hollow shield

Of lichen tough ; or bear, as silver bright,

Lunaria's pearly circlet, firm and light.

On the helm'd head the crimson foxglove glows,

Or Scutellaria guards the martial brows,

While the Leontodon its plumage rears,
And o'er the casque in waving grace appears ;
With stern undaunted eye, one warlike chief
Grasps the tall club from Arum's blood-dropt leaf
This, with the Burdock's hooks annoys his foes,
The purple thorn that borrows from the Rose.
In honeyed nectaries couched, some drive away
The forked insidious earwig from his prey ;
Fearless the scaled libellula assail,
Dart their keen lances at the encroaching snail ;
Arrest the winged ant, on pinions light,
And strike the headlong beetle in his flight.

Nor less assiduous round their lovely queen,
The lighter forms of female fays are seen ;

Rich was the purple vest Floscella wore,

Spun of the tufts the Tradescantia bore;

The Cistus' flowers minute her temple graced,

And threads of Yucca bound her slender waist.

From the wild bee, whose wond'rous labour weaves,

In artful folds the rose's fragrant leaves,

Was borrow'd fair Petalla's light cymar;

And the Hypericum, with spangling star,

O'er her fair locks its bloom minute enwreath'd;

Then, while voluptuous odours round her breath'd,

Came Nectarynia; as the arrowy rays

Of lambent fire round pictur'd seraphs blaze,

So did the Passiflora's radii shed,

Cerulean glory o'er the sylphid's head,

While round her form, the pliant tendrils twined,
And clasp'd the scarf that floated on the wind.

More grave the para-nymph Calyxa drest;
A brown transparent spatha formed her vest;
The silver scales that bound her raven hair,
Xeranthemum's unfading calyx bear;
And a light sash of spiral Ophrys press'd
Her filmy tunic, on her tender breast.

But where shall images or words be found
To paint the fair ethereal forms, that round
The queen of flowers attended? and the while
Bask'd in her eyes, and wanton'd in her smile.

Now towards the earth the gay procession bends,

Lo! from the buoyant air, the car descends;

Anticipating then the various year,

Flowers of all hues and every month appear,

From every swelling bulb its blossoms rise;

Here, blow the Hyacinths of loveliest dyes,

Breathing of heaven; and there, her royal brows

Begemmed with pearl, the Crown imperial shews;

Peeps the blue Gentian, from the soft'ning ground,

Jonquils and Violets, shed their odours round;

The Honeysuckle rears his scallop'd horn;

A snow of blossoms whiten on the thorn.

Here, like the fatal fruit to Paris given,

That spread fell feuds throughout the fabled heaven,

The yellow Rose her golden globe displays;

There lovelier still, among the spiny sprays

Her blushing rivals glow with brighter dyes,

Than paints the summer sun on western skies.

And the scarce tinged, and paler Rose unveil

Their modest beauties to the sighing gale.

Thro' the deep woodland's wild uncultur'd scene,

Spreads the soft influence of the floral queen;

See a fair pyramid the Chesnut rear,

Its crimson tassels on the Larch appear;

The Fir, dark native of the sullen North,

Owns her soft sway; and slowly springing forth

On the rough Oak are buds minute unfurl'd,

Whose giant produce may command the world!

Each forest thicket feels the balmy air,

And plants that love the shade are blowing there.

Rude rocks with Filices and Bryums smile,
And wastes are gay with Thyme and Chamomile.

Ah! yet prolong the dear delicious dream,
And trace her power along the mountain stream.
See! from its rude and rocky source, o'erhung
With female fern, and glossy adder's-tongue
Slowly it wells, in pure and chrystal drops,
And steals soft-gliding, thro' the upland copse;
Then murmuring on, along the willowy sides,
The reed-bird whispers, and the Halcyon hides;
While among sallows pale, and birchen bowers,
Embarks in Fancy's eye the queen of flowers.

O'er her light skiff, of woven bull-rush made,
The Water lily lends a polish'd shade;

While Galium there, of pale and silver hue,

And Epilobiums on the banks that grew,

Form her soft couch ; and as the Sylphs divide,

With pliant arms, the still increasing tide,

A thousand leaves along the stream unfold;

Amid its waving swords, in flaming gold

The Iris towers ; and here the Arrowhead

And water Crowfoot, more profusely spread

Spangle the quiet current ; higher there,

As conscious of her claims, in beauty rare,

Her rosy umbels rears the flow'ring Rush,

While with reflected charms the waters blush.

The naiad now, the year's fair goddess leads,

Through richer pastures and more level meads

Down to the sea; where even the briny sands

Their product offer to her glowing hands ;

For there, by sea-dews nurs'd and airs marine,

The Chelidonium blows ; in glaucous green,

Each refluent tide the thorn'd Eryngium laves,

And its pale leaves seem tinctured by the waves ;

And half-way up the cliff, whose rugged brow

Hangs o'er the ever toiling surge below,

Springs the light Tamarisk.—The summit bare,

Is tufted by the Statice ; and there,

Crush'd by the fisher, as he stands to mark

Some distant signal or approaching baık,

The Saltwort's starry stalks are thickly sown,

Like humble worth, unheeded and unknown !

From depths where corals spring from chrystal caves,

And break with scarlet branch, the eddying waves,

Where Algæ stream, as change the flowing tides,

And where, half flower, half fish, the Polyp hides,

And long tenacious bands of sea-lace twine

Round palm-shaped leaves impearl'd with coralline,

Enamour'd Fancy now the sea-maids calls,

And from their grottos dim, and shell-paved halls,

Charm'd by her voice, the shining train emerge,

And buoyant float above the circling surge;

Green Byssus, waving in the sea-born gales,

Form'd their thin mantles, and transparent veils,

Panier'd in shells, or bound with silver strings,

Of silken pinna; each her trophy brings

Of plants, from rocks and caverns submarine,

With leathery branch, and bladder'd buds between;

There, its dark folds the pucker'd laver spread,

With trees in miniature of various red;

H

There flag-shaped olive-leaves, depending hung,
And fairy fans from glossy pebbles sprung;
Then her terrestrial train the nereids meet,
And lay their spoils saline at Flora's feet.

O! fairest of the fabled forms! that stream,
Dress'd by wild Fancy, thro' the poet's dream,
Still may thy attributes of leaves and flowers,
Thy garden's rich, and shrub-o'ershadow'd bowers,
And yellow meads, with Spring's first honours bright,
The child's gay heart, and frolic step invite;
And, while the careless wanderer explores,
The umbrageous forest, or the rugged shores,
Climbs the green down, or roams the broom-clad waste,
May Truth, and Nature, form his future taste!
Goddess! on youth's bless'd hours thy gifts bestow;
Bind the fair wreath on virgin-beauty's brow,

And still may Fancy's brightest flowers be wove

Round the gold chains of hymeneal love.

But most for those, by Sorrow's hands oppress'd,

May thy beds blossom, and thy wilds be dress'd ;

And where by Fortune and the world forgot,

The mourner droops in some sequester'd spot,

(" Sad luxury to vulgar minds unknown,")

O'er blighted happiness for ever gone,

Yet the dear image seeks not to forget,

But woos his grief, and cherishes regret ;

Loving, with fond and lingering pain, to mourn

O'er joys and hopes that never will return ;—

Thou, visionary power ! mayst bid him view

Forms not less lovely, and as transient too ;

And while they soothe the wearied pilgrim's eyes,

Afford an antepast of Paradise.

STUDIES BY THE SEA.

Ah! wherefore do the incurious say,
    That this stupendous ocean wide,
No change presents from day to day,
    Save only the alternate tide;
Or save when gales of summer glide
    Across the lightly crisped wave;
Or, when against the cliff's rough side,
    As equinoctial tempests rave,
It wildly bursts; o'erwhelms the deluged strand,
Tears down its bounds, and desolates the land?

He who with more enquiring eyes
   Doth this extensive scene survey,
Beholds innumerous changes rise,
   As various winds its surface sway ;
Now o'er its heaving bosom play
   Small sparkling waves of silver gleam,
And as they lightly glide away
   Illume with fluctuating beam
The deepening surge ; green as the dewy corn
That undulates in April's breezy morn.

The far off waters then assume
   A glowing amethystine shade,
That changing like the peacock's plume,
   Seems in celestial blue to fade ;

Or paler, colder hues of lead,

  As lurid vapours float on high,

Along the ruffling billows spread,

  While darkly lours the threatening sky;

And the small scatter'd barks with outspread shrouds,

Catch the long gleams, that fall between the clouds.

Then day's bright star with blunted rays

  Seems struggling thro' the sea-fog pale,

And doubtful in the heavy haze,

  Is dimly seen the nearing sail;

'Till from the land a fresher gale

  Disperses the white mist, and clear,

As melts away the gauzy veil,

  The sun-reflecting waves appear;

So, brighter genuine virtue seems to rise
From envy's dark invidious calumnies.

What glories on the sun attend,
　　When the full tides of evening flow,
Where in still changing beauty, blend
　　With amber light, the opal's glow ;
While in the east the diamond bow
　　Rises in virgin lustre bright,
And from the horizon seems to throw,
　　A partial line of trembling light
To the hush'd shore ; and all the tranquil deep
Beneath the modest moon, is sooth'd to sleep.

Forgotten then, the thundering break
   Of waves, that in the tempest rise,
The falling cliff, the shatter'd wreck,
   The howling blast, the sufferer's cries ;
For soft the breeze of evening sighs,
   And murmuring seems in Fancy's ear
To whisper fairy lullabies,
   That tributary waters bear
From precipices, dark with piny woods,
And inland rocks, and heathy solitudes.

The vast encircling seas within,
   What endless swarms of creatures hide,
Of burnish'd scale, and spiny fin !
   These providential instincts guide,

And bid them know the annual tide,
  When, from unfathom'd waves that swell,
Beyond Fuego's stormy side,
  They come, to cheer the tribes that dwell
In Boreal climes; and thro' his half year's night
Give to the Lapland savage, food and light.

From cliffs, that pierce the northern sky,
  Where eagles rear their sanguine brood.
With long awaiting patient eye,
  Baffled by many a sailing cloud,
The Highland native marks the flood,
  Till bright the quickening billows roll,
And hosts of sea-birds, clamouring loud,
  Track with wild wing the welcome shoal,

Swift o'er the animated current sweep,
And bear their silver captives from the deep.

Sons of the North ! your streamy vales
　　With no rich sheaves rejoice and sing;
Her flowery robe no fruit conceals,
　　Tho' sweetly smile your tardy spring ;
Yet every mountain, clothed with ling,
　　Doth from its purple brow survey
Your busy sails, that ceaseless bring
　　To the broad frith,. and sheltering bay,
Riches, by Heaven's parental power supplied,—
The harvest of the far embracing tide.

And, where those fractur'd mountains lift
   O'er the blue wave their towering crest,
Each salient ledge and hollow cleft
   To sea-fowl give a rugged nest.
But with instinctive love is drest
   The Eider's downy cradle ; where
The mother-bird, her glossy breast
   Devotes, and with maternal care,
And plumeless bosom, stems the toiling seas,
That foam round the tempestuous Orcades.

From heights, whence shuddering sense recoils,
   And cloud-capped headlands, steep and bare,
Sons of the North ! your venturous toils
   Collect your poor and scanty fare.

Urged by imperious Want, you dare
  Scale the loose cliff, where Gannets hide,
Or scarce suspended, in the air
  Hang perilous ; and thus provide
The soft voluptuous couch, which not secures
To Luxury's pamper'd minions, sleep like yours.

Revolving still, the waves that now
  Just ripple on the level shore,
Have borne perchance the Indian's prow,
  Or half congeal'd, 'mid ice rocks hoar,
Raved to the Walrus' hollow roar ;
  Or have by currents swift convey'd
To the cold coast of Labrador,
  The relics of the tropic shade ;

And to the wondering Esquimaux have shown
Leaves of strange shape, and fruits unlike their own.

No more then, let the incurious say,
No change this world of water shows,
But as the tides the moon obey,
Or tempests rave, or calms repose.—
Shew them, its bounteous breast bestows
On myriads life ; and bid them see
In every wave that circling flows,
Beauty and use, and harmony—
Works of the Power Supreme, who poured the flood,
Round the green peopled earth, and call'd it good !

THE HOROLOGE OF THE FIELDS.

*Addressed to a Young Lady, on seeing at the House of an
Acquaintance a magnificent French Timepiece.*

For her who owns this splendid toy,
    Where use with elegance unites,
Still may its index point to joy,
    And moments wing'd with new delights.

Sweet may resound each silver bell,—
    And never quick returning chime,
Seem in reproving notes to tell,
    Of hours mispent, and murder'd time.

Tho' Fortune, Emily, deny
  To us these splendid works of art,
The woods, the lawns, the heaths supply
  Lessons from Nature to the heart.

In every copse, and shelter'd dell,
  Unveil'd to the observant eye,
Are faithful monitors, who tell
  How pass the hours and seasons by.

The green robed children of the Spring
  Will mark the periods as they pass,
Mingle with leaves Time's feather'd wing,
  And bind with flowers his silent glass.

Mark where transparent waters glide,
  Soft flowing o'er their tranquil bed;
There, cradled on the dimpling tide,
  Nymphæa rests her lovely head.

But conscious of the earliest beam,
  She rises from her humid rest,
And sees reflected in the stream
  The virgin whiteness of her breast.

Till the bright daystar to the west
  Declines, in Ocean's surge to lave,
Then folded in her modest vest,
  She slumbers on the rocking wave.

See Hieracium's various tribe,
 Of plumy seed and radiate flowers,
The course of Time their blooms describe,
 And wake or sleep appointed hours.

Broad o'er its imbricated cup
 The Goatsbeard spreads its golden rays,
But shuts its cautious petals up,
 Retreating from the noon-tide blaze:

Pale as a pensive cloister'd nun
 The Bethlem-star, her face unveils,
When o'er the mountain peers the Sun,
 But shades it from the vesper gales.

I

Among the loose and arid sands
    The humble Arenaria creeps ;
Slowly the purple star expands,
    But soon within its calyx sleeps.

And those small bells so lightly ray'd
    With young Aurora's rosy hue,
Are to the noon-tide Sun display'd,
    But shut their plaits against the dew.

On upland slopes the shepherds mark
    The hour, when as the dial true,
Cichorium to the towering Lark,
    Lifts her soft eyes, serenely blue.

And thou " Wee crimson tipped flower,"
  Gatherest thy fringed mantle round
Thy bosom, at the closing hour,
  When night drops bathe the turfy ground.

Unlike Silene, who declines
  The garish noontide's blazing light ;
But when the evening crescent shines,
  Gives all her sweetness to the night.

Thus in each flower and simple bell,
  That in our path untrodden lie,
Are sweet remembrancers who tell
  How fast the winged moments fly.

I 2

Time will steal on with ceaseless pace,
Yet lose we not the fleeting hours,
Who still their fairy footsteps trace,
As light they dance among the flowers.

SAINT MONICA.

Among deep woods is the dismantled scite

Of an old Abbey, where the chaunted rite,

By twice ten brethren of the monkish cowl,

Was duly sung; and requiems for the soul

Of the first founder: For the lordly chief,

Who flourish'd paramount of many a fief,

Left here a stipend yearly paid, that they,

The pious monks, for his repose might say

Mass and orisons to Saint Monica.

Beneath the falling archway overgrown
With briars, a bench remains, a single stone,
Where sat the indigent, to wait the dole
Given at the buttery ; that the baron's soul
The poor might intercede for ; there would rest,
Known by his hat of straw with cockles drest,
And staff and humble weed of watchet gray,
The wandering pilgrim ; who came there to pray
'The intercession of Saint Monica.

Stern Reformation and the lapse of years
Have reft the windows, and no more appears
Abbot or martyr on the glass anneal'd ;
And half the falling cloisters are conceal'd

By ash and elder : the refectory wall
Oft in the storm of night is heard to fall,
When, wearied by the labours of the day,
The half awaken'd cotters, starting say,
" It is the ruins of Saint Monica."

Now with approaching rain is heard the rill,
Just trickling thro' a deep and hollow gill
By osiers, and the alder's crowding bush,
Reeds, and dwarf elder, and the pithy rush,
Choak'd and impeded : to the lower ground
Slowly it creeps ; there traces still are found
Of hollow squares, embank'd with beaten clay,
Where brightly glitter'd in the eye of day
The peopled waters of Saint Monica.

The chapel pavement, where the name and date,
Or monkish rhyme, had mark'd the graven plate,
With docks and nettles now is overgrown;
And brambles trail above the dead unknown.——
Impatient of the heat, the straggling ewe
Tinkles her drowsy bell, as nibbling slow
She picks the grass among the thistles gray,
Whose feather'd seed the light air bears away,
O'er the pale relicks of Saint Monica.

Reecho'd by the walls, the owl obscene
Hoots to the night; as thro' the ivy green
Whose matted tods the arch and buttress bind,
Sobs in low gusts the melancholy wind:

The Conium there, her stalks bedropp'd with red,
Rears, with Circea, neighbour of the dead;
Atropa too, that, as the beldams say,
Shews her black fruit to tempt and to betray,
Nods by the mouldering shrine of Monica.

Old tales and legends are not quite forgot.
Still Superstition hovers o'er the spot,
And tells how here, the wan and restless sprite,
By some way-wilder'd peasant seen at night,
Gibbers and shrieks, among the ruins drear;
And how the friar's lanthorn will appear
Gleaming among the woods, with fearful ray,
And from the church-yard take its wavering way,
To the dim arches of Saint Monica.

The antiquary comes not to explore,

As once, the unrafter'd roof and pathless floor;

For now, no more beneath the vaulted ground

Is crosier, cross, or sculptur'd chalice found,

Nor record telling of the wassail ale,

What time the welcome summons to regale,

Given by the matin peal on holiday,

The villagers rejoicing to obey,

Feasted, in honour of Saint Monica.

Yet often still at eve, or early morn,

Among these ruins shagg'd with fern and thorn,

A pensive stranger from his lonely seat

Observes the rapid martin, threading fleet

The broken arch : or follows with his eye,
The wall-creeper that hunts the burnish'd fly ;
Sees the newt basking in the sunny ray,
Or snail that sinuous winds his shining way,
O'er the time-fretted walls of Monica.

He comes not here, from the sepulchral stone
To tear the oblivious pall that Time has thrown,
But meditating, marks the power proceed
From the mapped lichen, to the plumed weed,
From thready mosses to the veined flower,
The silent, slow, but ever active power
Of Vegetative Life, that o'er Decay
Weaves her green mantle, when returning May
Dresses the ruins of Saint Monica.

Oh Nature! ever lovely, ever new,

He whom his earliest vows has paid to you

Still finds, that life has something to bestow ;

And while to dark Forgetfulness they go,

Man, and the works of man ; immortal Youth,

Unfading Beauty, and eternal Truth,

Your Heaven-indited volume will display,

While Art's elaborate monuments decay,

Even as these shatter'd aisles, deserted Monica !

A WALK IN THE SHRUBBERY.

To the Cistus or Rock Rose, a beautiful plant, whose flowers
expand, and fall off twice in twenty-four hours.

THE Florists, who have fondly watch'd,
  Some curious bulb from hour to hour,
And, to ideal charms attach'd,
  Derive their glory from a flower;

Or they, who lose in crouded rooms,
  Spring's tepid suns and balmy air,
And value Flora's fairest blooms,
  But in proportion as they 're rare;

Feel not the pensive pleasures known
   To him, who, thro' the morning mist,
Explores the bowery shrubs new blown,
   A moralizing Botanist.——

He marks, with colours how profuse
   Some are design'd to please the eye;
While beauty some combine with use,
   In admirable harmony.

The fruit buds, shadow'd red and white,
   Amid young leaves of April hue;
Convey sensations of delight,
   And promise fruits autumnal too:

And, while the Thrush his home and food,
  Hails, as the flowering thorns unfold,
And from its trunk of ebon wood,
  Rears Cytisus its floating gold ;

The Lilac, whose tall head discloses
  Groups of such bright empurpled shade,
And snow-globes form'd of elfin roses,
  Seem for exclusive beauty made :

Such too art thou ; when light anew
  Above the eastern hill is seen,
Thy buds, as fearful of the dew,
  Still wear their sheltering veil of green.

But in the next more genial hour
   Thy tender rose-shaped cups unfold,
And soon appears the perfect flower,
   With ruby spots and threads of gold.

That short and fleeting hour gone by,
   And even the slightest breath of air,
Scarce heard among thy leaves to sigh,
   Or little bird that flutters there;

Shakes off thy petals thin and frail,
   And soon, like half-congealing snow,
The sport of every wandering gale,
   They strew the humid turf below.

Yet tho' thy gauzy bells fall fast,
  Long ere appears the evening crescent;
Another bloom succeeds the last,
  As lovely and as evanescent.

Not so the poet's favourite Rose,
  She blooms beyond a second day,
And even some later beauty shews—
  Some charm still lingering in decay.

Thus those, who thro' life's path have pass'd,
  A path how seldom strewn with flowers !
May have met Friendships formed to last
  Beyond the noonday's golden hours.

K

While quickly formed, dissolv'd as soon,
  Some warm attachments I have known
Just flourish for an hour at noon,
  But leave no trace when overblown.

Minds that form these, with ardent zeal
  Their *new* connexions fondly cherish,
And for a moment keenly feel
  Affection, doomed as soon to perish;

Incapable of Friendship long,
  Awake to every new impression,
Old friends, becoming *ci-devant !*
  Are still replaced by a Succession.

HOPE.

A RONDEAU.

Parody on Lord Strangford's " Just like Love."

Just like Hope is yonder bow,
   That from the center bends so low,
Where bright prismatic colours shew
   How gems of heavenly radiance glow,

     Just like Hope!

Yet if, to the illusion new,
   The pilgrim should the arch pursue,
Farther and farther from his view,
   It flies; then melts in chilling dew,

     Just like Hope!

   K 2

Ye fäde, ethereal hues ! for ever,

While, cold Reason, thy endeavour

Sooths not that sad heart, which never

      Glows with Hope.

EVENING.

Oh! soothing hour, when glowing day,
   Low in the western wave declines,
And village murmurs die away,
   And bright the vesper planet shines ;

I love to hear the gale of Even
   Breathing along the new-leaf'd copse,
And feel the freshening dew of Heaven,
   Fall silently in limpid drops.

For, like a friend's consoling sighs,

   That breeze of night to me appears ;

And, as soft dew from Pity's eyes,

   Descend those pure celestial tears.

Alas ! for those who long have borne,

   Like me, a heart by sorrow riven,

Who, but the plaintive winds, will mourn,

   What tears will fall, but those of Heaven ;

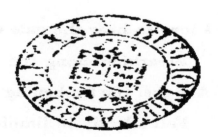

LOVE AND FOLLY,

FROM THE FABLES OF LA FONTAINE.

Love, who now deals to human hearts,
Such ill thrown, yet resistless darts,
   That hapless mortals can't withstand them,
Was once less cruel and perverse,
Nor did he then his shafts disperse,
           So much at random.

It happened, that the thoughtless child
Was rambling thro' a flowery wild,
    Like idle lad in school vacation;
Where sauntering now, and now at rest,
Stroll'd Folly, who to Love address'd
               His conversation.

On trifles he had much to say,
Then laughing he propos'd to play,
    And stake against Love's bow his bauble;
The quiver'd gamester smil'd and won,
But testy Folly soon began
              To fret and squabble.

Loud and more loud the quarrel grows;

From words the wranglers went to blows,

For Folly's rage is prompt to rise;

Till bleeding Love a martyr stood—

A stroke from Folly's weapon rude,

Put out his eyes.

Then wild with anguish, Venus pray'd,

For vengeance on the idiot's head,

And begg'd of cloud-compelling Jove,

His swiftest lightening, to destroy,

The mischievous malignant boy

That blinded Love.

" Folly is immortal," Jove replied,

" But, tho' your prayer must be denied,

   " An endless penance is decreed him ;

" For *Love*, tho' blind, will reign around

" The world ; but still where-ever found,

            " *Folly* shall lead him."

ON THE APHORISM,

" L'Amitié est l'Amour sans ailes."

FRIENDSHIP, as some sage poet sings,
Is chasten'd Love, depriv'd of wings,
Without all wish or power to wander;
Less volatile, but not less tender:
Yet says the proverb—" Sly and slow
" Love creeps, even where he cannot go ;"
To clip his pinions then is vain,
His old propensities remain ;

And she, who years *beyond fifteen*,
Has counted *twenty*, may have seen
How rarely unplum'd Love will stay;
He flies not—but he coolly walks away.

NOTES.

NOTES.

BEACHY HEAD.

Page 1.   Line 3.

" The mariner at early morning hails."

In crossing the Channel from the coast of France, Beachy-Head is the first land made.

Page 1.   Line 6.

" Of vast concussion, when the Omnipotent

" Stretch'd forth his arm ———"

Alluding to an idea that this Island was once joined to the continent of Europe, and torn from it by some

convulsion of Nature.   I confess I never could trace
the resemblance between the two countries.   Yet the
cliffs about Dieppe, resemble the chalk cliffs on the
Southern coast.   But Normandy has no likeness
whatever to the part of England opposite to it.

Page 2.   Line 15.

Terns.——Sterna hirundo, or Sea Swallow.

Gulls.——Larus canus.

Tarrocks.——Larus tridactylus.

Page 3.   Line 1.

Gray Choughs.——Corvus Graculus, Cornish Choughs,
or, as these birds are called by the Sussex people,
Saddle-backed Crows, build in great numbers on this
coast.

Page 4.   Line 10.

" Bursts from its pod the vegetable down."
Cotton.   (Gossypium herbaceum.)

Line 14.

" The beamy adamant." Diamonds, the hardest
and most valuable of precious stones.

For the extraordinary exertions of the Indians
in diving for the pearl oysters, see the account of the
Pearl Fisheries in Percival's View of Ceylon.

Page 8.   Line 14.

" ——— But now and then the Sea Snipe's cry,"&c.

In crossing the channel this bird is heard at night,
uttering a short cry, and flitting along near the surface of the waves.   The sailors call it the Sea Snipe;

L

but I can find no species of sea bird of which this is the vulgar name. A bird so called inhabits the Lake of Geneva.

Page 9.

" The period, when from Neustria's hostile shore
  The Norman launch'd his galleys, and the bay
  O'er which that mass of ruin* frowns even now
  In vain and sullen menace, then received
  The new invaders," &c.

The Scandinavians†, and other inhabitants of the north, began towards the end of the 8th century, to leave their inhospitable climate in search of the produce of more fortunate countries.

---

* Pevensey Castle.
† Scandinavia.—Modern Norway, Sweden, Denmark, Lapland, &c.

The North-men made inroads on the coasts of France; and carrying back immense booty, excited their compatriots to engage in the same piratical voyages : and they were afterwards joined by numbers of necessitous and daring adventurers from the coasts of Provence and Sicily.

In 844, these wandering innovators had a great number of vessels at sea; and again visiting the coasts of France, Spain, and England, the following year they penetrated even to Paris : and the unfortunate Charles the Bald, king of France, purchased at a high price, the retreat of the banditti he had no other means of repelling.

These successful expeditions continued for some time; till Rollo, otherwise Raoul, assembled a number of followers, and after a descent on England, crossed the channel, and made himself master of Rouen, which he fortified. Charles the Simple, unable to contend with Rollo, offered to resign to him some of the northern provinces, and to give him his daughter in marriage. Neustria, since called Normandy, was granted to him, and afterwards Brittany. He added the more solid virtues of the legislator to the fierce valour of the conqueror—converted to Christianity, he established justice, and repressed the excesses of his Danish subjects, till then accustomed to live only by plunder. His name became the signal for pursuing those who violated the laws ; as well as the cry of Haro, still so usual in Normandy. The Danes and Francs produced a race of men celebrated for their valour; and it was a small party of these that in 983, having been on a pilgrimage to Jerusalem, arrived on their return at Salerno, and found the town surrounded by Mahometans, whom the Salernians were bribing to leave their coast. The Normans represented to them the baseness and cowardice of such submission; and notwithstanding the inequality of their numbers, they boldly attacked the Saracen camp, and drove the infidels to their ships. The prince of Salerno, astonished at their successful audacity, would have loaded them with the marks of his gratitude; but refusing every reward, they returned to their own country, from whence, however, other bodies of Normans passed into Sicily*; and many of them entered into the service of the emperor of the East, others of the Pope,

* Anciently called Trinacria.

and the duke of Naples was happy to engage a small party of them in defence of his newly founded dutchy. Soon afterwards three brothers of Coutance, the sons of Tancred de Hauteville, Guillaume Fier-a-bras, Drogon, and Humfroi, joining the Normans established at Aversa, became masters of the fertile island of Sicily; and Robert Guiscard joining them, the Normans became sovereigns both of Sicily and Naples*. How William, the natural son of Robert, duke of Normandy, possessed himself of England, is too well known to be repeated here. William sailing from St. Valori, landed in the bay of Pevensey; and at the place now called Battle, met the English forces under Harold: an esquire (ecuyer) called Taillefer,

---

* Parthenope.

mounted on an armed horse, led on the Normans, singing in a thundering tone the war song of Rollo. He threw himself among the English, and was killed on the first onset. In a marsh not far from Hastings, the skeletons of an armed man and horse were found a few years since, which are believed to have belonged to the Normans, as a party of their horse, deceived in the nature of the ground, perished in the morass.

Page 10.   Line 10.

" Then the holy pile," &c.

Battle Abbey was raised by the Conqueror, and endowed with an ample revenue, that masses might be said night and day for the souls of those who perished in battle.

Page 11.   Last line.

" Thou, leagued with the Batavian—."

In 1690, king William being then in Ireland, Tour-
ville, the French admiral, arrived on the coast of England.   His fleet consisted of seventy-eight large ships,
and twenty-two fire-ships. Lord Torrington, the English
admiral, lay at St. Helens, with only forty English
and a few Dutch ships; and conscious of the disad-
vantage under which he should give battle, he ran
up between the enemy's fleet and the coast, to pro-
tect it.   The queen's council, dictated to by Russel,
persuaded her to order Torrington to venture a battle.
The orders Torrington appears to have obeyed re-
luctantly: his fleet now consisted of twenty-two
Dutch and thirty-four English ships.   Evertson, the
Dutch admiral, was eager to obtain glory; Torring-

ton, more cautious, reflected on the importance of the stake. The consequence was, that the Dutch rashly sailing on were surrounded, and Torrington, solicitous to recover this false step, placed himself with difficulty between the Dutch and French ;— but three Dutch ships were burnt, two of their admirals killed, and almost all their ships disabled. The English and Dutch declining a second engagement, retired towards the mouth of the Thames. The French, from ignorance of the coast, and misunderstanding among each other, failed to take all the advantage they might have done of this victory.

Page 13.

" ——— ————— the humble home
Of one, who sometimes watches on the heights," &c.

The shepherds and labourers of this tract of country, a hardy and athletic race of men, are almost universally engaged in the contraband trade, carried on
for the coarsest and most destructive spirits, with
the opposite coast. When no other vessel will venture to sea, these men hazard their lives to elude the
watchfulness of the Revenue officers, and to secure
their cargoes.

Page 14. Line 15.

" Where the gemm'd sun-dew grows, or fring'd buck-bean,
They scare the plover———"

    Sun-dew.——Drosera rotundifolia
    Buck-bean.——Menyanthes trifoliatum.
    Plover.——Tringa vanellus.

Page 15. Line 9.

" By crouding osiers, and the black coot hides—"

Coot.—Fulica aterrima.

Line 16.

" With blossom'd furze, unprofitably gay."

Goldsmith.

Page 16. Line 7.

" Hostile war-fires." The Beacons formerly lighted up on the hills to give notice of the approach of an enemy. These signals would still be used in case of alarm, if the Telegraph now substituted could not be distinguished on account of fog or darkness.

Line 11.

" Where clamouring loud, the evening curlew runs."

Curlew.—Charadrius œdicnemus.

Page 20.

" ————————— where Vecta breaks

With her white rocks, the strong imperious tide."

Vecta.—The Isle of Wight, which breaks the force of the waves when they are driven by south-west winds against this long and open coast. It is somewhere described as " Vecta shouldering the Western Waves."

Page 22. Line 3.

" By the rude arms of trees, lovely in spring."

Every cottage in this country has its orchard; and I imagine that not even those of Herefordshire, or Worcestershire, exhibit a more beautiful prospect, when the trees are in bloom, and the " Primavera candida e vermiglia," is every where so enchanting.

Page 24. Line 10.

" Where purple tassels of the tangling vetch—"
Vetch.—Vicia sylvatica.

Line 11.

" With bittersweet, and bryony inweave."
Bittersweet—Solanum dulcamara.
Bryony.—Bryonia alba.

Line 12.

" And the dew fills the silver bindweed's cups—"
Bindweed.—Convolvulus sepium.

Line 14.

" Nourish the harebell, and the freckled pagil."
Harebell.—Hyacinthus non scriptus.
Pagil.—Primula veris.

Page 25.   Line 5.

" Plucks the wood sorrel—"

Oxalis acetosella.

Line 8.

" Gathers, the copse's pride, anémones."

Anemóne nemorosa.—It appears to be settled on late and excellent authorities, that this word should not be accented on the second syllable, but on the penultima. I have however ventured the more known accentuation, as more generally used, and suiting better the nature of my verse.

Page 26.   Line 3.

" Of sea-shells ; with the pale calcareous soil

   Mingled, and seeming of resembling substance."

Among the crumbling chalk I have often found shells, some quite in a fossil state and hardly distinguishable from chalk. Others appeared more recent; cockles, muscles, and periwinkles, I well remember, were among the number; and some whose names I do not know. A great number were like those of small land snails. It is now many years since I made these observations. The appearance of sea-shells so far from the sea excited my surprise, though I then knew nothing of natural history. I have never read any of the late theories of the earth, nor was I ever satisfied with the attempts to explain many of the phenomena which call forth conjecture in those books I happened to have had access to on this subject.

Page 26. Line 11.

" Or did this range of chalky mountains," &c.

The theory here slightly hinted at, is taken from an idea started by Mr. White.

Page 27. Last line.

" Rest the remains of men, of whom is left—"

These Downs are not only marked with traces of encampments, which from their forms are called Roman or Danish; but there are numerous tumuli among them. Some of which having been opened a few years ago, were supposed by a learned antiquary to contain the remains of the original natives of the country.

Page 28. Line 8.

" Where the mail'd legions, under Claudius," &c.

That the legions of Claudius were in this part of Britain appears certain. Since this emperor re-

ceived the submission of Cantii, Atrebates, Ireno-
bates, and Regni, in which latter denomination were
included the people of Sussex.

Page 28.

" What time the huge unwieldy elephant
  Auxiliary reluctant, hither led——"

In the year 1740, some workmen digging in the
park at Burton in Sussex, discovered, nine feet below
the surface, the teeth and bones of an elephant; two
of the former were seven feet eight inches in length.
There were besides these, tusks, one of which broke in
removing it, a grinder not at all decayed, and a part
of the jaw-bone, with bones of the knee and thigh,
and several others. Some of them remained very
lately at Burton House, the seat of John Biddulph,
Esq. Others were in possession of the Rev. Dr.

M

Langrish, minister of Petworth at that period, who
was present when some of these bones were taken up,
and gave it as his opinion, that they had remained
there since the universal deluge.   The Romans under
the Emperor Claudius probably brought elephants into
Britain.   Milton, in the Second Book of his History,
in speaking of the expedition, says that "He like
a great eastern king, with armed elephants, marched
through Gallia."   This is given on the authority of
Dion Cassius, in his Life of the Emperor Claudius.
It has therefore been conjectured, that the bones found
at Burton might have been those of one of these elephants, who perished there soon after its landing; or
dying on the high downs, one of which, called Dunc-
ton Hill, rises immediately above Burton Park, the
bones might have been washed down by the torrents

of rain, and buried deep in the soil. They were not found together, but scattered at some distance from each other. The two tusks were twenty feet apart. I had often heard of the elephant's bones at Burton, but never saw them; and I have no books to refer to. I think I saw, in what is now called the National Museum at Paris, the very large bones of an elephant, which were found in North America : though it is certain that this enormous animal is never seen in its natural state, but in the countries under the torrid zone of the old world. I have, since making this note, been told that the bones of the rhinoceros and hippopotamus have been found in America.

Page 28.   Line 16.

" —— and in giants dwelling on the hills ——"

The peasants believe that the large bones sometimes found belonged to giants, who formerly lived on
the hills.   The devil also has a great deal to do with
the remarkable forms of hill and vale : the Devil's
Punch Bowl, the Devil's Leaps, and the Devil's
Dyke, are names given to deep hollows, or high and
abrupt ridges, in this and the neighbouring county.

Page 29.   Line 8.

" The pirate Dane, who from his circular camp—"
The incursions of the Danes were for many ages the
scourge of this island.

Line 12.

" The savage native, who his acorn meal—"
The Aborigines of this country lived in woods, un-
sheltered but by trees and caves ; and were probably

as truly savage as any of those who are now termed so.

Page 30. Line 10.

" Will from among the fescue bring him flowers—"

The grass called Sheep's Fescue, (Festuca ovina,) clothes these Downs with the softest turf.

"———————————— some resembling bees

In velvet vest intent on their sweet toil—"

Ophrys apifera, Bee Ophrys, or Orchis; found plentifully on the hills, as well as the next.

Line 13.

" While others mimic flies, that lightly sport—"

Ophrys muscifera.—Fly Orchis. Linnæus, misled by the variations to which some of this tribe are really subject, has perhaps too rashly esteemed all those which resemble insects, as forming only one species, which he terms Ophrys insectifera.   See English Botany.

Page 31.   Line 3.

" Blue bells wave tremulous.——"

    (Campanula rotundifolia.)

" ——————————————————— The mountain thyme Purples the hassock of the heaving mole."

Thymus serpyllum. " It is a common notion, that the flesh of sheep which feed upon aromatic plants, particularly wild thyme, is superior in flavour to other mutton.   The truth is, that sheep do not crop these aromatic plants, unless now and then by accident, or when they are first turned on hungry to downs, heaths, or commons ; but the soil and situations favourable to aromatic plants, produce a short sweet pasturage, best adapted to feeding sheep, whom nature designed for mountains, and not for turnip grounds and rich meadows. The attachment of bees to this, and other aromatic plants, is well known." Martyn's Miller.

Line 5.

" And the short turf is gay with tormentil."
Tormentilla reptans.

" And bird's foot trefoil, and the lesser tribes
  Of hawkweed ; spangling it with fringed stars.——"
Bird's foot trefoil.——Trifolium ornithopoides.
Hawkweed.——Hieracium, many sorts.

Line 11.

" The guardian of the flock, with watchful care,——"

The downs, especially to the south, where they are less abrupt, are in many places under the plough; and the attention of the shepherds is there particularly required to keep the flocks from trespassing.

Page 31. Line 13.

" While his boy visits every wired trap—"

Square holes cut in the turf, into which a wire noose is fixed, to catch Wheatears. Mr. White says, that these birds (Motacilla œnanthe) are never taken beyond the river Adur, and Beding Hill; but this is certainly a mistake.

Line 15.

' The timid migrants, who from distant wilds,—"

These birds are extremely fearful, and on the slightest appearance of a cloud, run for shelter to the first rut, or heap of stones, that they see.

Page 32.

" ———————————— the Shepherd still protects
'The social bird, who from his native haunts—"

The Yellow Wagtail.—Motacilla flava. It frequents the banks of rivulets in winter, making its nest in meadows and corn-fields. But after the breeding season is over, it haunts downs and sheepwalks, and is seen constantly among the flocks, probably for the sake of the insects it picks up. In France the shepherds call it *La Bergeronette*, and say it often gives them, by its cry, notice of approaching danger.

Page 33.

" —————————— a gnarled thorn,

Bent by the sea blast,—"

The strong winds from the south-west occasion al-most all the trees, which on these hills are exposed to it, to grow the other way.

Line 3.

" ————————— how wide the view !"

So extensive are some of the views from these hills, that only the want of power in the human eye to travel so far, prevents London itself being dis-cerned. Description falls so infinitely short of the reality, that only here and there, distinct features can be given.

Line 9.

" Of Kentish hills,——"

A scar of chalk in a hill beyond Sevenoaks in Kent, is very distinctly seen of a clear day.

Line 11.

" And airy summits,——"

The hills about Dorking in Surry; over almost the whole extent of which county the prospect extends.

Line 13.

" Of Black-down shagg'd with heath,——"

This is an high ridge, extending between Sussex and Surry. It is covered with heath, and has almost always a dark appearance. On it is a telegraph.

Page 34.   Line 2.

" The portal and the ruin'd battlements—"

In this country there are several of the fortresses
or castles built by Stephen of Blois, in his contention
for the kingdom, with the daughter of Henry the
First, the empress Matilda.   Some of these are now
converted into farm houses.

Page 35.   Line 5.

" Or night-jar, chasing fern-flies.——"

Dr. Aikin remarks, I believe, in his essay " On
the Application of Natural History to the Purposes
of Poetry," how many of our best poets have no-
ticed the same circumstance, the hum of the Dor
Beetle (Scarabœus stercorarius,) among the sounds
heard by the evening wanderer.   I remember only

one instance in which the more remarkable, though by no means uncommon noise, of the Fern Owl, or Goatsucker, is mentioned. It is called the Night Hawk, the Jar Bird, the Churn Owl, and the Fern Owl, from its feeding on the Scarabœus solstitialis, or Fern Chafer, which it catches while on the wing with its claws, the middle toe of which is long and curiously serrated, on purpose to hold them. It was this bird that was intended to be described in the Forty-second Sonnet (Smith's Sonnets). I was mistaken in supposing it as visible in November; it is a migrant, and leaves this country in August. I had often seen and heard it, but I did not then know its name or history. It is called Goatsucker (Caprimulgus), from a strange prejudice taken against it by the Italians, who assert that it sucks their goats;

botanists.   The Cuckoo flower is the Lychnis flos-cuculi.

Page 41.   Line 6.

Flag-flower.—Iris pseudacorus.

Page 42.   Line 9.

Yaffils.—Woodpeckers (Picus); three or four species in Britain.

Page 43.   Line 5.

" And gales that close—"

" And liquid notes that close the eye of day."

Milton.

The idea here meant to be conveyed is of the evening wind, so welcome after a hot day of Summer, and which appears to sooth and lull all nature into tranquillity.

Page 44. Line 3.

" But the gay bird of blushing breast."

The Robin, (Motacilla rubecula,) which is always heard after other songsters have ceased to sing.

Line 4.

" And Woodlarks still will haunt the shade."
The Woodlark, (Alauda nemorosa,) sings very late.

Line 6.

Reed-wrens, (Motacilla arundinacea,) sing all the summer and autumn, and are often heard during the night.

Page 47. Line 3

" May haply build," &c.

An allusion to the visionary delights of the new.

N

discovered islands, where it was at first believed
men lived in a state of simplicity and happiness;
but where, as later enquiries have ascertained, that
exemption from toil, which the fertility of their
country gives them, produces the grossest vices; and
a degree of corruption that late navigators think will
end in the extirpation of the whole people in a few
years.

Line 14.

" Dwelt one," &c.

In a cavern almost immediately under the cliff
called Beachy Head, there lived, as the people of the
country believed, a man of the name of Darby, who
for many years had no other abode than this cave,
and subsisted almost entirely on shell-fish. He had

often administered assistance to ship-wrecked mariners; but venturing into the sea on this charitable mission during a violent equinoctial storm, he himself perished. As it is above thirty years since I heard this tradition of Parson Darby (for so I think he was called): it may now perhaps be forgotten.

Page 48. Line 9.

" Betrayed not then the little careless sheep."

Sometimes in thick weather the sheep feeding on the summit of the cliff, miss their footing, and are killed by the fall.

Page 49. Line 5.

" Or the dark porpoises."

Delphinus phocœna.

NOTES TO THE FABLES.

These are old stories, which I have endeavoured to tell with such a degree of novelty as natural history can lend them. They have been so often repeated, that probably the original inventors have been long since forgotten. La Fontaine, whose graceful simplicity in such light narrative has been universally allowed, is the most usually referred to.

La Fontaine, in his manner of telling the story of Les deux Pigeons, calls them *Friends*. But the proverbial conjugal fidelity of this race of birds, makes it seem more natural to describe them as the pigeon and his mate. If it be objected, that the Truant Dove is represented as repeating the apology of Henry the Fourth of France—" Toujours perdrix, toujours Chapon bouilli ne vaut rien ;" and that his partner talks from Shakspeare; I must take refuge under the authority of Chaucer; or rather his polisher Dryden; who makes his Dame Partlet quote Galen and Cato, while Chanticleer explains Latin sentences:

" For in the days of yore the birds of parts,
    Were bred to speak and sing; and learn the liberal
        arts."

In fact, if the mind momentarily acquiesces in the absurdity of animals having the passions and the faculties of man, every thing else may be granted.

It might be necessary to apologize for inserting these fables; but that which Prior and Cowper, and so many other of the most eminent writers have not disdained, can never need any defence.

La Fontaine begins the second Fable here inserted thus :

"L'Alouette et ses Petits, avec le Maître d'un Champ.

Ne t'attends qu'à toi seul, c'est un commun proverbe ;

Voici comme Esope le mit

En credit."

There is nothing I am more desirous of avoiding, even in a trifle like this, than the charge of plagiarism.   I must in the present instance defend myself by stating, that so long since as April 1805, Mr. Johnson was in possession of the MS. copy of this Fable.   In July 1806, a friend brought with her from London, a volume called "The Birds of Scotland, with other Poems," in which I read, what, if my fable had been first published, I might perhaps have thought very like an imitation.   My lines of the Lark are :

"————————————————— But like a dart

From his low homested with the morning springs,

And far above the floating vapour sings,

At such an height,

That even the shepherd lad upon the hill,

Hearing his matin note so shrill,

With shaded eyes against the lustre bright,

Scarce sees him twinkling in a *flood of light*—"

Mr. Graham, in a more lengthened description, says of the Lark :

" ———————————————— He towers

In loftier poise, with sweeter fuller pipe,

Cheering the ploughman at his furrow end,

The while he clears the share ; or listening, leans

Upon his paddle staff ; and with rais'd hand

Shadows his half-shut eyes, striving to scan

The songster melting in the *flood of light*—"

The extreme resemblance of these passages may be accounted for, however, by the observation very justly made, that natural objects being equally visible to all, it is very probable that descriptions of such objects will be often alike.

I cannot help remarking another coincidence. My lines on the female Lark sitting, are :

> " She leaves her nest reluctant and in haste,
>
> And scarce allows herself to taste
>
> A dew drop and a few small seeds—"

Mr. Graham says of the Wren :

> " ——————————————— never flitting off,
>
> Save when the morning Sun is high, to drink
>
> A dew drop from the nearest flower cup—"

ADDITIONAL NOTES TO THE FABLES.

The varieties of pigeons here named, as Fantail, Carrier, Pouter, Almond Tumbler, and Nun, with many others, are varieties produced by art from the common pigeon. Societies exist in which prizes are given to those who produce birds nearest to the standard of imaginary perfection. A Pouter is a bird of which the crop is capable of being so much distended with wind, that the animal appears to be without a head. On this enlargement of the crop depends the beauty and value of the bird.

These Fanciers are to Ornithologists, what Flower Fanciers are to Botanists.

NOTES ON THE SWALLOW.

Page 79.   Line 1.

The Gorse-Furze.—Ulex Europæus.   Called so in many counties of England.

Line 2.

" The banks with speedwell flowers are gay."

Veronica chamœdrys.—This elegant flower, though not celebrated like the Primrose, Cowslip, and Daisy, is in all its varieties one of the most beautiful of our indigenous plants.

Page 80.   Line 6.

" As fables tell, an Indian Sage —"

There are two or three fables that relate the knowledge acquired by some Indian recluse, of the language of birds.

*

Page 81.   Line 8.

The Cuckoo, the Rail, and many species of Doves, are all emigrants.

> " Were you in Asia ? O relate,
>
> If there your fabled sister's woes
>
> She seem'd in sorrow to relate,
>
> Or sings she but to celebrate
>
> Her nuptials with the Rose ?"

Alluding to the Ovidian fable of the Metamorphosis of Procne and Philomela into the Swallow and the Nightingale ; and to the oriental story of the Loves of the Nightingale and the Rose ; which is told with such elegant extravagance in the Botanic Garden.

Page 82.   Line 4.

" And come to build anew among —"

Accurate observers have remarked, that an equal

number of these birds return every year to build in the places they frequented before; and that each pair set immediately about repairing a particular nest.

Page 82.

" You hide, tho' none know where or how,

In the cliff's excavated brow," &c.

Many persons have supported the idea, that the Hirundines linger concealed among rocks and hollows in a torpid state, and that all do not emigrate.

Page 83.

" Or if, by instinct taught to know

Approaching dearth of insect food,

To isles and willowy aits you go."

Another opinion is, that the Swallows, at the time they disappear, assemble about rivers and ponds, and a number of them settling on the pliant boughs of willow and osier, sink by their weight into the water; at the bottom of which they remain torpid till the ensuing spring. For the foundation of these various theories, see " White's History of Selbourne."

NOTES TO FLORA.

Page 85. Line 5.

" Whose first prerogative," &c. *V. Cowper.*

" The spleen is seldom felt where Flora reigns—
The lowering eye, the petulance, the frown,
And sullen sadness, that do shade, distort,
And mar the face of Beauty, when no cause
For such immeasurable grief appears,
These Flora banishes."

Page 86.   Line 9.

Saxifraga hypnoides.—Moss Saxifrage, commonly called Ladies' Cushion.

Line 13.

" The tufted rush," &c.

Eriophorum angustifolium.

Page 87.   Line 3.

" And wild convolvuli," &c.

Convolvulus arvensis.—A remarkably pretty plant, but no favourite with the husbandman.

Line 7.

" The rest were by the Scandix' points confin'd—"

Scandix pecten.—Venus' comb, or Shepherd's needle.

Line 10.

" She waved the Anthoxanthum in her hand."

Anthoxanthum odoratum.——Vernal Meadow Grass.

It is to this grass that hay owes its fine odour.

Page 88.   Line 8.

" And brush the aphis," &c.

Aphis, or Aphides.——These are the " myriads brushed from Russian wilds ;" the blights, cankers, lice, or vermin, to use common phrases, that so often disfigure, and destroy the fairest vegetable productions.

Line 11.

" Of Lichen tough."

Lichen.——Of these many have the forms of shields, when in fructification.

Page 88.   Line 12.

" Lunaria's pearly circlet."

Lunaria annua.—Moonwort, usually called Honesty.

ine   13.

" —— the crimson foxglove glows."

Digitalis purpurea.

Line 14.

" Or Scutellaria guards," &c.

Scutellaria galericulata.—Small skull-cap.

Page 89.   Line 1.

" While the Leontodon," &c.

Leontodon officinalis.—Common Dent-de-lion.

Page 89.　Line 4.

" —— from Arum's blood-dropt leaf."

Arum maculatum—Vulgarly Cuckoo pint, or Lords and Ladies.

Line 5.

" This, with the Burdock's hooks," &c.
Arctium lappa.

Line 9.

" Fearless the scaled libellula," &c.

The Dragon-fly, or as it is called in the southern countries, the Horse-stinger, though it preys only on other insects. Several sorts of these are seen about water; but its introduction here is a poetical licence, as it does not feed on, or injure flowers.

o

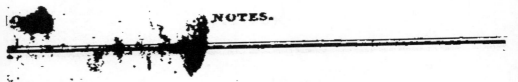

Page 90.   Line 2.

" Spun of the tufts the Tradescantia bore."

Tradescantia virginica.——The silk-like tuft within this plant appears to the eye composed of very fine filaments ; but on examining one of these small silky threads through a microscope, it looks like a string of Amethysts.

Line 3.

" The Cistus' flowers," &c.

Cistus helianthemum.   Dwarf Cistus.

Line 4.

" And threads of Yucca," &c.

Yucca filamentosa.

Page 90. Line 5.

" From the wild bee," &c.

Apis centuncularis. This insect weaves, or rather cements rose leaves together, to form its cell.

Line 8.

" And the Hypericum," &c.

An elegant shrub, of which Cowper thus speaks :

" Hypericum all bloom, so thick a swarm

 Of flowers, like flies clothing her slender rods,

That scarce a leaf appears."

It seems admirably adapted to a fairy garland.

Line 13.

" So did the Passiflora's radii shed."

Passiflora cerulea.

Page 91.   Line 4.

" A brown transparent spatha," &c.

The sheath from which many flowers spring, such as the Narcissus, &c.

Line 6.

" Xeranthemum's unfading calyx bear."

The scales of one species of the Xeranthemum are particularly elegant.

Line 7.

" ———— of spiral Ophrys," &c.

Ophrys spiralis.—Ladies traces.

The following lines describing well known flowers, notes would be superfluous.

. Page 94.   Line 6.

" With female fern."——

Polypodium filix fœmina.

Page 94. Line 6.

"And glossy adder's-tongue."

Asplenium scolopendrium.

Line 10.

"The reed-bird whispers."

Motacilla salicaria. The Reed Sparrow, or Willow Wren. A bird that in a low and sweet note imitates several others, and sings all night.

"And the Halcyon hides."

Alcedo hispida.—The Kingsfisher, or Halcyon, one of the most beautiful of English birds.

Line 14.

"The Water-lily lends," &c.

Nymphæa alba.

Page 95.   Line 1.

" While Galium there," &c.

Galium palustre.——White Ladies' bedstraw.

Line 2.

Epilobiums.——Willow herbs——various species.

Line 7.

" The Iris towers."

Iris palustris.——Yellow Iris.

" ——— and here the Arrowhead," &c.

Sagittaria sagittifolia.

Line 8.

" And water Crowfoot," &c.

Ranunculus aquaticus.

Line 11.

" Her rosy umbels rears the flow'ring Rush."

Butomus umbellatus. The only native of England of the class Enneandria.

Page 96.   Line 2.

" The Chelidonium blows."

Chelidonium glaucium.   The horned or sea Poppy.

Line 3.

" ——— the thorn'd Eryngium," &c.

Eryngium maritimum.——Sea Holly.

Line 7.

" Springs the light Tamarisk."

Tamarix gallica.   This elegant plant is not very uncommon on cliffs in the West of England, and was in 1800 to be found on an high rock to the eastward of the town of Hastings in Sussex.

Page 96. Line 8.

" Is tufted by the Statice."

Statice armeria.—Sea Pink, Sea Lavender, commonly called Thrift, is frequently used for borders of flower-beds.   It covers some of the most sterile cliffs.

Line 11.

" The Saltwort's starry stalks."

Salsola kali.   This plant when burnt affords a fossile alkali, and is used in the manufacture of glass. The best is brought from the Mediterranean, and forms a considerable article of commerce.   It is very frequent on the cliffs on the Sussex coast.

Page 97. Line 1.

" Where Algæ stream," &c.

The Algæ include all the sea plants, and some other aquatics.

Page 97. Line 2.

" ———— the Polyp hides," &c.

The Polypus or Sea Anemone. Coralline is, if I do not misunderstand the only book I have to consult, a shelly substance, the work of sea insects, adhering to stones and to sea-weeds.

Line 9.

" Green Byssus," &c.

Flos aquæ.—Paper byssus ; a semitransparent substance floating on the waves.

Line 12.

" Of silken Pinna," &c.

The Pinna, or Sea Wing, is contained in a two-valved shell. It consists of fine long silk-like fibres. The Pinna on the coast of Provence, and Italy, is called the Silk-worm of the Sea. Stockings and gloves of exquisite fineness have been made of it. See note 27, to the Economy of Vegetation.

The subsequent lines attempt a description of Sea Plants, without any correct classification.

NOTES TO STUDIES BY THE SEA.

Page 104. Line 6.

" And murmuring seems in Fancy's ear."

Whoever has listened on a still summer or autumnal evening, to the murmurs of the small waves, just breaking on the shingles, and remarked the low sounds reechoed by the distant rocks, will understand this.

Page 105. Line 1.

" And bid them know the annual tide."

The course of those wonderful swarms of fishes that take their annual journey is, I believe, less understood than the emigration of birds. I suppose them, without having any particular ground for my conjecture, to begin their voyage from beyond the extreme point of the southern continent of America. Many of the northern nations live almost entirely on fish. Their light, during the long night of an arctic winter, is supplied by the oil of marine animals.

Page 105.   Line 11.

" The Highland native marks the flood."

In the countries where the produce of the sea is so
necessary to human life, the arrival of shoals of fish
is most eagerly waited for by the hardy inhabitant.
Thrown on the summit of an high cliff, overlooking
the sea, the native watches for the approach of the
expected good, and sees with pleasure the numerous
sea-birds, who by an instinct superior to his own,
perceive it at a far greater distance, and follow to
take their share of the swarming multitude.

Page 106.   Line 7.

" Yet every mountain, clothed with ling."

Ling.—A name given in many parts of England
to the Erica vulgaris, or Common Heath.

Page 107. Line 6.

" The Eider's downy cradle."

Anas mollissima. While many sea-birds deposit their eggs on the bare rocks, the Eider duck lines her nest most carefully with the feathers from her own breast, which are particularly fine and light : the nest is robbed, and she a second time unplumes herself for the accommodation of her young. If the lining be again taken away, the drake lends his breast feathers ; but if after that, their unreasonable persecutors deprive it of its lining, they abandon the nest in despair, the master of the domicile wisely judging, that any further sacrifice would be useless.

Page 108. Line 2.

" Scale the loose cliff where Gannets hide."

Pelicanus bassanus. The Gannet builds on the highest rocks.

Line 3.

" Or scarce suspended, in the air

Hang perilous."

Suspended by a slight rope, the adventurous native of the north of Scotland is let down from the highest cliffs that hang over the sea, while with little or no support, he collects the eggs of the sea fowl, in a basket tied round his waist. The feathers also of these birds gathered from the rocks are a great object. to these poor industrious people.

Line 11.

" Rav'd to the Walrus' hollow roar."

Trichecus rosmarus.—The Walrus or Morse; a creature of the Seal kind, now said to be no longer found on the coast of Scotland, but still inhabiting other northern countries. They are sometimes eighteen or twenty feet long, and they roar like bulls.

Line 12.

" Or have by currents," &c.

Gulph currents are supposed to throw the remains of fruits of the tropical regions on the most northern coast of America; and it is asserted that the same fruits are also found on the coast of Norway. See " Les Etudes de la Nature."

NOTES ON THE HOROLOGE OF THE FIELDS.

The sleep of plants has been frequently the subject of inquiry and admiration.

" Vigiliæ Plantarum.—Botanists, under this term, comprehend the precise time of the day in which the flowers of different plants open, expand, and shut.   As all plants do not flower in the same season, or month ; in like manner, those which flower the same day in the same place, do not open and shut precisely at the same hour.   Some open in the morning, as the lipped flowers, and compound flowers with flat spreading petals ; others at noon, as the mallows ; and a third set in the evening, or after sun-set, as some Geraniums and Opuntias.   The hour of shutting is equally determined.   Of those which open in the morning, some shut soon after, while others remain expanded till night." For further information on this subject, see Milne's Botanical Dictionary.

Page 112.   Line 4.

Nymphæa alba.—The flower of this beautiful aquatic opens about seven in the morning, closes about four in the afternoon, and then lies down upon the surface of the water.   *Linnæus.*

Page 113.   Line 1.

" Hieracium's various tribe."

All I believe of the solar tribe ; the two mentioned by Withering are the sabaudum and murorum. The first opens at seven, and shuts between one and two ; the other expands at six in the morning, and closes between two and three in the afternoon.

P

Page 113.   Line 6.

" The Goat'sbeard," &c.

Tragopogon pratense.—A most unfortunate name for poetry. The yellow sort, which is the most common, opens about three in the morning, and closes between nine and ten. *Withering*.

Line 10.

" The Bethlem-star," &c.

Ornithogalum umbellatum.

Page 114.   Line 2.

Arenaria marina.—Flowers open at nine o'clock in the morning, and shut between two and three in the afternoon. *Lightfoot*'s Flora Scotica.

Page 114. Line 6.

" And those small bells so lightly ray'd

With young Aurora's rosy hue—"

Convolvulus arvensis.—The flowers close in the evening.

Line 11.

Cichorium intybus.—Wild Succory, Cichory, or Endive. The flowers open at eight o'clock in the morning, and close at four in the afternoon.

Withering.

Page 115. Line 1.

" And thou ' Wee crimson-tipped flower.' "

Quoted from Burn's address to the mountain daisy. The flowers close at night.

Page 115.   Line 5.

Silene noctiflora.—" Flowers opening in the night, sweet-scented in the summer, not so in the autumn."

Withering's Botany.

NOTES ON SAINT MONICA.

Page 119.   Line 7.

" Just trickling thro' a deep and hollow gill."

Gill is a word understood in many parts of England, and more particularly in the North, to mean an hollow watercourse, or an hollow overshadowed with coppice and brush wood, such as frequently occur in hilly countries.   It has the same meaning as Gully, a deep trench in the earth, so frequent in the West Indies, where the tropic rains tear away the earth and make hollows, which in process of time become overgrown with trees, and the resort of monkeys and other animals.

Page 120.

" —————— The Ivy green

Whose matted tods," &c.

A judicious friend objected to this expression as obscure; but it has the authority of Spencer.

" At length within an *Ivy tod*

There shrouded was the little God."

Shepherd's Calendar. Ecl. 3.

And I think I could quote other poets as having used it.

Page 121.　Line 1.

Conium maculatum.

Line 3.

Atropa belladonna.

Line 10.

" Gibbers and shrieks," &c.

The word Gibber has been also objected to; but besides that it appears to me very expressive, I have for its use the example of Shakspeare:

" ———————————— the sheeted dead

Did squeal and *gibber* in the streets of Rome."

Hamlet.

Page 123.　Line 2.

" The Wall-creeper that hunts the burnish'd fly."

Certhia muraria.—This bird frequents old towers, castles, and walls; feeding on insects.

Page 123. Line 3.

" Sees the newt basking," &c..

Lacerta vulgaris.—This reptile in its complete state lives among rubbish and old walls. It is the Wall Newt of Shakspeare, as part of the food of poor Tom:

" The wall newt and the water newt,

With rats and mice and such small deer,

Have been Tom's food for many a year."

And is commonly known by the name of Evett or Eft; and from its ugliness is held in abhorrence, and is supposed to be venomous, though perfectly harmless.

NOTES TO A WALK IN THE SHRUBBERY.

The extravagant fondness for the cultivation of those flowers which the art of the gardener can improve, such as Tulips, Auriculas, and Carnations, has excited laughter and contempt; and was, I think, sometimes confounded with the Science of Botany, with which it has little to do. A Florist, however, has very different pursuits and purposes from a Botanist.

Cistus ladaniferus.—Gum cistus. This plant took its trivial name from its having been supposed to produce the ladanum of the shops, and ought to have been changed when the mistake was detected.

Page 127. Line 4.

Cytisus laburnum. This beautiful tree, of which there are many sorts, attains great perfection in this country. The wood is black, of a fine grain, and takes a polish like Ebony. The French call it from thence, L'Ebene; the Ebony tree.

Line 7.

" And snow-globes form'd of elfin roses.

Viburnum, commonly called Guelder Rose.—A shrub of great beauty, of which the globular groups are composed of single monopetalous flowers: it is a cultivated variety of the Viburnum opulus, Water-elder of the hedges, sometimes called The Wayfaring Tree.

NOTES ON LOVE AND FOLLY.

This is called the most elegant of the Fables of **La** Fontaine, though it is perhaps told with less simplicity than is generally his perfection.   But the close is admirable.

> " Quand on eut bien considéré
>
> L'interêt du public, celui de la patrie,
>
> Le résultat enfin de la suprême cour
>
> Fut, de condamner la Folie
>
> A servir de guide à l'Amour."

Page 136.   Line 9.

" **And stake against Love's bow his bauble.**"

When kings and great men, to divert the tedious

hours of those who have nothing to do, kept about them a fool, one who either really was deficient in understanding, or abject enough to pretend to a degree of idiotism for the amusement of his patron; the insignia of the office were, a cap with feathers, or sometimes a cock's head fastened to the top, and with bells round it, while in their hands was carried a short wooden truncheon, on which was rudely carved a human head with asses ears. There are several passages describing this in Johnson's or Stevens' Notes on Shakspeare.

ERRATA.

Page 41, line 12, for *bows* read *boughs.*
——— 46, ——— 6, insert *Amanda.*

THE END.

Lately published,

BY THE SAME AUTHOR.

———

1. CONVERSATIONS, with POETRY; chiefly on Subjects of Natural History. For the Use of Young People. 2 Vols. Price 7s.

2. And speedily will be published, A HISTORY OF BIRDS, for the Use of Young People, in 2 Vols.

Printed by W. Pople,
22, Old Boswell Court, Strand.

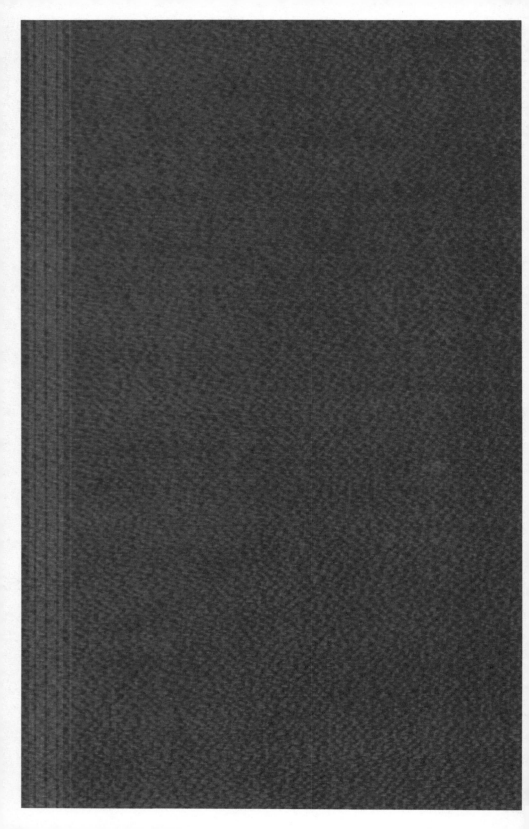

WS - #0195 - 240624 - C0 - 229/152/14 - PB - 9781406974218 - Gloss Lamination